Great Taste ~ Lo

LIGHT BEEF & PORK

TIME
LIFE
BOOKS

ALEXANDRIA, VIRGINIA

TABLE OF CONTENTS

Pork Sauté with Chive Cream Sauce

page 62

Grilled Beef Teriyaki

～

page 115

INTRODUCTION

Our mission at Great Taste-Low Fat is to take the work and worry out of everyday low-fat cooking; to provide delicious, fresh, and filling recipes for family and friends; to use quick, streamlined methods and available ingredients; and, within every recipe, to keep the percentage of calories from fat under 30 percent.

The American way of serving meat is an eye-opener to people from other parts of the world: Restaurants here proudly offer an oversize steak or a massive rack of ribs that hangs off the edges of the plate, with the only vegetables in sight a sprig of parsley and perhaps a mountain of onion rings or french fries. But most of us have come to realize that that's hardly a healthful way to eat.

BEEF AND PORK FOR TODAY

Nobody's saying you should stop eating meat. But we do suggest rethinking the proportions of meals that center on meat. Rather than a 12-ounce steak or a 2-inch-thick chop as the main attraction, consider dishes like these: rice pilaf studded with kidney beans and cubes of pork; a tamale casserole of chilied pork with a cornmeal crust; beef braises and stews served over generous portions of pasta; and pork kebabs with onions, tomatoes, and pineapple, served on a bed of couscous. It doesn't sound like you'll leave the table hungry, does it?

Even when meat makes up a fairly substantial part of the meal—when chops or ribs or a burger take center stage—we've found ways to keep the meals low in fat. One obvious option is to use the leanest cuts available, and to trim all fat from the meat before cooking. And of course we employ cooking methods that require little or no added fat: pan-frying in a nonstick skillet, broiling, grilling, and baking. You'll never see a skimpy-looking plate in this book; each well-filled dish is a satisfying combination of beef or pork and pasta, grains, breadstuffs (such as tortillas or pita pockets), and plenty of fresh vegetables.

ALWAYS SOMETHING NEW

Rather than a monotonous weekly round of steaks, chops, and roasts, the recipes in this book supply a tempting assortment of ideas for quick, easy meals. The five chapters are organized by cooking technique: Braises & Stews, Stir-Fries & Sautés, Oven Dishes, On the Grill, and Salads. The first chapter exploits classic slow-cooking methods with recipes such as Sicilian-Style Braised Beef, Pork Stew with Pasta and Caramelized Onions, Beef Stew with Apples and Ginger, and Three-Alarm Pork and Beef Chili. Quick, dependable routes to great meals, stir-frying and sautéing are ideal ways to cook pork and beef. Try the superb Steak au Poivre with Peppers and Potatoes, Pan-Fried Beef Stroganoff, exotic Moroccan Spiced Pork Sauté, and homey Beef and Macaroni Skillet Dinner. Our Oven Dishes take you on an international culinary tour, with stops in Italy (for Baked Pork Manicotti), Greece (for Beef Moussaka), the Middle East (Pork, Ham, and Rice Pilaf), and Mexico (Pork Enchiladas); there's robust American fare here as well—dishes like Baked Cincinnati Chili and Oven-Barbecued Pork Tenderloin. Whether grilling is a summertime treat or a year-round pleasure where you live, our On the Grill recipes give you good reason to plan a cookout. In addition to steak and burgers (try Grilled Mustard-Coated Beef or Pork Burgers with Sweet Potato Relish), you'll find less familiar creations, such as Grilled Pork Satay (Southeast Asian-style skewered meat), Grilled Beef Teriyaki, and Tandoori Pork Kebabs. Eating pleasure by the bountiful bowlful is the theme of the Salads chapter. Choose from Pork Taco Salad, Oven-Barbecued Pork with Corn and Watercress Salad, Thai-Style Beef Salad with Noodles, and many more.

Even if you've been cooking meat for years, there's lots to be learned from our "Secrets of Low-Fat Cooking" section, where we bring you up to date on the ingredients and techniques that add up to more healthful meat cookery. You'll discover ingredients that "extend" meat, making it a more substantial meal, and get some tips on full-flavored seasonings. Finally, we supply step-by-step photographs explaining how to prepare meat for cooking and how to slice it when it's done. Get started today—there's some rib-sticking great eating in your future!

CONTRIBUTING EDITORS

Sandra Rose Gluck, *a New York City chef, has years of experience creating delicious low-fat recipes that are quick to prepare. Her secret for satisfying results is to always aim for great taste and variety. By combining readily available, fresh ingredients with simple cooking techniques, Sandra has created the perfect recipes for today's busy lifestyles.*

Grace Young *has been the director of a major test kitchen specializing in low-fat and health-related cookbooks for over 12 years. Grace oversees the development, taste testing, and nutritional analysis of every recipe in Great Taste-Low Fat. Her goal is simple: take the work and worry out of low-fat cooking so that you can enjoy delicious, healthy meals every day.*

Kate Slate *has been a food editor for almost 20 years, and has published thousands of recipes in cookbooks and magazines. As the Editorial Director of Great Taste-Low Fat, Kate combined simple, easy to follow directions with practical low-fat cooking tips. The result is guaranteed to make your low-fat cooking as rewarding and fun as it is foolproof.*

NUTRITION

Every recipe in *Great Taste-Low Fat* provides per-serving values for the nutrients listed in the chart at right. The daily intakes listed in the chart are based on those recommended by the USDA and presume a nonsedentary lifestyle. The nutritional emphasis in this book is not only on controlling calories, but on reducing total fat grams. Research has shown that dietary fat metabolizes more easily into body fat than do carbohydrates and protein. In order to control the amount of fat in a given recipe and in your diet in general, no more than 30 percent of the calories should come from fat.

Nutrient	Women	Men
Fat	<65 g	<80 g
Calories	2000	2500
Saturated fat	<20 g	<25 g
Carbohydrate	300 g	375 g
Protein	50 g	65 g
Cholesterol	<300 mg	<300 mg
Sodium	<2400 mg	<2400 mg

These recommended daily intakes are averages used by the Food and Drug Administration and are consistent with the labeling on all food products. Although the values for cholesterol and sodium are the same for all adults, the other intake values vary depending on gender, ideal weight, and activity level. Check with a physician or nutritionist for your own daily intake values.

SECRETS OF LOW-FAT COOKING

LIGHT BEEF AND PORK

The challenge in creating healthy meals with beef and pork is to balance the quantity of meat with generous amounts of ingredients that are lower in fat—satisfying starches, such as rice and pasta, as well as vegetables. You'll also need to boost the seasonings, because fat carries flavor, and when fat is removed, flavors can pale. Finally, be careful never to overcook lean meat, which, without protective fat, can easily turn tough and dry.

LEANER THAN EVER

The beef and pork sold in American markets today are considerably leaner than they were in the past. Selective breeding has lowered the fat content of pork more than 30 percent since the early 1980s; in the same period, the fat content of beef has dropped more than 25 percent. In addition, beef processors are trimming retail cuts more closely, so beef comes to the market with less external fat. Always trim any remaining external fat before cooking beef or pork.

When selecting meat for your meals, it helps to be familiar with the leaner cuts. In general, the loin (the back, behind the ribs) of either animal is the best source of meat that is tender and flavorful, yet lean. With beef, the round, or rear section of the steer, and the flank (just behind the belly) are two other sources of lean meat. Most of the pork recipes in this book call for pork loin or tenderloin; the beef recipes are made with sirloin, top round, or flank steak.

Beef grades can also help direct you toward the leanest meat. Beef for retail sale may be (it's not mandatory) graded by government inspectors, who categorize the meat as Prime, Choice, or Select; Prime is the fattiest and Select the leanest. (There is no grading system for pork.)

Not all supermarkets sell government-graded beef, so you should learn to judge fat content by eye: Lean beef resembles the flank steak and top round shown in the photo at right—predominantly solid muscle that is not marbled through with veins of fat. In addition, beef should be a clear red (pork should be pink to pinkish-gray, with pork loin and tenderloin darker in color than other cuts). The meat should feel springy to the touch, and external fat should be creamy white, not yellow.

MAKING A MEAL

When the portion of meat is scaled down, you need to choose accompaniments wisely so that the meal is still satisfying. Carbohydrate-rich foods, such as potatoes, beans, corn, pasta, and grains, are your smartest options. It's not just that these foods are both low in fat and filling, they also absorb the flavors of the meat, giving the impression that there's more beef or pork in the dish than there actually is.

To prepare meat for cooking, we often use marinades, which penetrate the surface of the meat, locking in flavor. If acid ingredients such as vinegar are used, the marinade also functions to some extent as a meat tenderizer. For deeper flavor, you can often marinate the meat longer than the recipe specifies (up to 8 hours), but you should refrigerate it. Stock up on a variety of oils and vinegars: Olive and sesame oils, and wine, cider, and rice vinegars are the basics for marinades.

Basting sauces are another flavor enhancer for broiled, grilled, or roasted meat. Bottled barbecue sauce and condiments such as mustard, chili sauce, and salsa simplify sauce-making. Seasoning rubs and spreads also work wonders: These mixtures of assertive ingredients such as garlic, scallions, herbs, spices, pepper, mustard, and lemon zest are applied to the meat before cooking.

The concentrated flavors of dried fruits and sun-dried tomatoes bring a spark to savory braises and meat-and-grain dishes; fresh herbs lend a distinctive finishing touch to sauces and salads.

Preparing Meat for Cooking

When you buy meat at the supermarket, the fat will already have been trimmed quite closely (to less than ⅛ inch, down from ¾ inch in the 1980s). But you can take the next step and trim the meat even more closely to remove all separable fat. Use a small, sharp knife, and try not to cut into the lean interior of the meat (this would allow juices to escape during cooking).

Ground beef labels have changed, but they can still be confusing: Ground beef labeled "lean" has 18 grams of fat per 3½-ounce cooked portion—more than *four times* the fat found in well-trimmed top round. So we suggest buying a lean cut of beef (or pork) and chopping it in a food processor. All you have to do is cut the meat into chunks, place it in a food processor, and process until finely ground; pulsing the machine on and off gives you maximum control.

Cutting beef and pork into thin or small pieces enables you to sauté or stir-fry it in the shortest possible time—and quick cooking is one of the keys to keeping lean meat tender and juicy. Beef and pork can also be pounded to create elegant individual portions that will cook in a flash. Step-by-step directions are at right.

Custom-Cutting Beef and Pork

When sautéing or stir-frying boneless beef or pork, you'll need to cut the meat into thin slices or small strips. The photographs below show you how to do this. The cutting will go more smoothly if your knife is good and sharp.

To cut thin strips of beef for stir-frying, first chill the meat (this is top round) in the freezer for about 15 minutes to firm it up. Then with a long, sharp knife, cut the steak in half horizontally, using a sawing motion.

Separate the two pieces of meat (return them briefly to the freezer, if necessary, to refirm them). Then cut each piece crosswise (across the grain) into thin strips; our recipes call for strips that are either ½ or ¼ inch thick.

To cut scallops of pork tenderloin, first chill the pork in the freezer for about 15 minutes to firm it up. Then, with a sharp knife, cut the pork crosswise into slices that are about ½ inch thick.

The pork scallops can then be cut into thin strips for stir-frying. Return the meat briefly to the freezer, if necessary, to refirm it, then cut each piece crosswise (across the grain) into ¼-inch-thick strips.

Pounding Cutlets or Steak

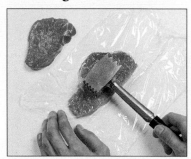

Pounding slices of beef or pork to an even thickness helps them cook quickly. Place the meat between two sheets of plastic wrap or waxed paper and with the flat side of a meat pounder or a small skillet, pound the meat to a uniform ½- to ⅛-inch thickness.

"Tenderizing" Flank Steak

Slicing cooked flank steak across the grain and on the diagonal shortens the meat fibers, making the steak more tender. When you need bite-size pieces (for a salad, for example), first cut the steak in half, with the grain; then thinly slice it crosswise.

BRAISES & STEWS
1

BEEF STEW WITH BRANDY-MUSTARD SAUCE

SERVES: 4
WORKING TIME: 25 MINUTES
TOTAL TIME: 40 MINUTES

What begins as a basic beef stew takes on French flair with the addition of brandy and Dijon mustard. The brandy is briefly cooked to concentrate its compelling flavor, which permeates the vegetables. The mustard is stirred in shortly before serving as a delicious finishing touch. A salad made with tart greens, such as watercress, is the perfect accompaniment for this rich stew.

2 tablespoons flour

½ teaspoon salt

½ teaspoon freshly ground black pepper

10 ounces well-trimmed beef sirloin, cut into ½-inch chunks

1 tablespoon olive oil

8 ounces fettuccine, broken into thirds

4 scallions, thinly sliced

2 cloves garlic, slivered

3 carrots, halved lengthwise and cut into 1-inch lengths

½ pound mushrooms, quartered

¼ cup brandy

1½ cups reduced-sodium beef broth, defatted

2 tablespoons no-salt-added tomato paste

⅓ cup evaporated low-fat milk

4 teaspoons Dijon mustard

1. On a sheet of waxed paper, combine the flour, ¼ teaspoon of the salt, and ¼ teaspoon of the pepper. Dredge the beef in the flour mixture, shaking off and reserving the excess. In a large skillet or Dutch oven, heat the oil until hot but not smoking over medium heat. Add the beef and cook, stirring frequently, until browned, about 4 minutes. With a slotted spoon, transfer the beef to a plate.

2. In a large pot of boiling water, cook the pasta until just tender. Drain well. Meanwhile, add the scallions, garlic, carrots, and mushrooms to the skillet and cook, stirring frequently, until the vegetables are lightly browned, about 4 minutes. Remove the pan from the heat, pour in the brandy, and return the pan to the heat. Increase the heat to high and cook until the brandy is almost evaporated, about 2 minutes.

3. Add the broth and tomato paste to the pan and bring to a boil. Reduce to a simmer, cover, and cook, stirring frequently, until the carrots are tender, about 15 minutes. In a small bowl, combine the evaporated milk and reserved flour mixture, whisking to blend. Stir into the skillet along with the mustard, the remaining ¼ teaspoon salt, and remaining ¼ teaspoon pepper. Return the beef to the pan and cook, stirring, until the sauce is slightly thickened and no floury taste remains, about 2 minutes. Divide the pasta among 4 plates, top with the stew, and serve.

FAT: 10G/20%
CALORIES: 441
SATURATED FAT: 2.1G
CARBOHYDRATE: 57G
PROTEIN: 28G
CHOLESTEROL: 100MG
SODIUM: 735MG

What a meal! We've taken slices of sirloin steak, pounded them thin, filled them with an herbed bread-and-cheese stuffing, and then rolled them up, jelly-roll style. They're sliced thin and served over pasta and are topped with a tangy citrus-tomato sauce. Julienned summer squash, steamed and tossed with sliced scallions, makes a great accompaniment.

Sicilian-Style Braised Beef

SERVES: 4
WORKING TIME: 20 MINUTES
TOTAL TIME: 35 MINUTES

8 ounces orzo pasta

⅓ cup golden raisins, coarsely chopped

¼ cup plain dried bread crumbs

¼ cup grated Parmesan cheese

½ cup chopped fresh basil

2 cloves garlic, minced

¾ teaspoon fennel seeds, lightly crushed

½ teaspoon grated orange zest

½ teaspoon freshly ground black pepper

¼ teaspoon salt

10 ounces well-trimmed beef sirloin, cut into 4 slices and pounded (see page 8) ⅛ inch thick

2 tablespoons flour

1 tablespoon olive oil

½ cup orange juice

2 cups no-salt-added canned tomatoes, chopped with their juices

½ cup reduced-sodium beef broth, defatted

1. In a large pot of boiling water, cook the pasta until just tender. Drain well.

2. Meanwhile, in a small bowl, combine the raisins, bread crumbs, Parmesan, ¼ cup of the basil, the garlic, fennel seeds, orange zest, pepper, and salt. Sprinkle the mixture over the beef slices, then roll them up (see tip). Secure with toothpicks.

3. Dredge the beef rolls in the flour, shaking off the excess. In a large nonstick skillet, heat the oil until hot but not smoking over medium heat. Add the beef rolls, seam-sides down, and cook until lightly browned, about 1 minute. Turn seam-sides up, add the orange juice to the skillet, and cook until slightly reduced, about 2 minutes. Add the tomatoes, broth, and the remaining ¼ cup basil and bring to a boil. Reduce to a simmer, cover, and cook until the beef is cooked through and the sauce is richly flavored, about 12 minutes.

4. Cut each beef roll crosswise into 6 slices. Divide the pasta among 4 plates, top with the beef slices, spoon the sauce over, and serve.

Helpful hint: With a sawing motion, use a thin, sharp knife to cut the beef rolls into slices.

FAT: 10G/19%
CALORIES: 480
SATURATED FAT: 2.8G
CARBOHYDRATE: 70G
PROTEIN: 28G
CHOLESTEROL: 47MG
SODIUM: 429MG

TIP

Leave some space around the edges when you coat the beef slices with the bread crumb mixture. Then roll them up from one short end and secure with toothpicks.

Sweet and Sour Braised Pork Patties

SERVES: 4
WORKING TIME: 20 MINUTES
TOTAL TIME: 30 MINUTES

This meal of piquantly sauced pork patties and vegetables served over hot, fluffy rice may seem like a lot of work—you chop the pork yourself and the tricolor medley of vegetables is fresh, not frozen or canned—but it's not. The method is streamlined and the intriguing flavors are created with pantry-shelf ingredients, including mustard, ketchup, wine vinegar, and soy sauce.

1 cup long-grain rice

½ teaspoon salt

10 ounces well-trimmed pork tenderloin, cut into chunks

2 slices (2 ounces total) firm-textured white bread, crumbled

3 scallions, thinly sliced

3 tablespoons ketchup

1 tablespoon reduced-sodium soy sauce

1 teaspoon Dijon mustard

2 teaspoons olive oil

2 tablespoons flour

1 red bell pepper, cut into ½-inch squares

¼ pound green beans, cut into 1-inch lengths

1 yellow summer squash, cut into ½-inch cubes

1¼ cups reduced-sodium chicken broth, defatted

2 tablespoons red wine vinegar

2 teaspoons sugar

¼ teaspoon red pepper flakes

1½ teaspoons cornstarch mixed with 1 tablespoon water

1. In a medium saucepan, bring 2¼ cups of water to a boil. Add the rice and ¼ teaspoon of the salt, reduce to a simmer, cover, and cook until the rice is tender, about 17 minutes.

2. Meanwhile, in a food processor, process the pork until finely ground, about 1 minute. Transfer the pork to a large bowl and stir in the bread, scallions, 1 tablespoon of the ketchup, the soy sauce, mustard, and the remaining ¼ teaspoon salt. Mix well and shape into 4 oval patties.

3. In a large nonstick skillet, heat the oil until hot but not smoking over medium heat. Dredge the patties in the flour, shaking off the excess. Cook the patties until lightly browned, about 2 minutes per side. Transfer the patties to a plate.

4. Add the bell pepper, green beans, and squash to the skillet and cook, stirring, until the vegetables are lightly browned, about 4 minutes. Add the broth, vinegar, sugar, red pepper flakes, and the remaining 2 tablespoons ketchup. Bring to a boil and reduce to a simmer. Return the pork to the pan, cover, and cook until the patties are cooked through and the vegetables are tender, about 10 minutes. Add the cornstarch mixture and cook, stirring, until slightly thickened, about 1 minute. Divide the rice among 4 plates, spoon the patties and vegetable mixture over, and serve.

FAT: 6G/14%
CALORIES: 385
SATURATED FAT: 1.3G
CARBOHYDRATE: 60G
PROTEIN: 22G
CHOLESTEROL: 46MG
SODIUM: 881MG

PORK STEW WITH CREAMY PEANUT SAUCE

SERVES: 4
WORKING TIME: 20 MINUTES
TOTAL TIME: 35 MINUTES

2 tablespoons flour

¾ teaspoon salt

½ teaspoon freshly ground black pepper

10 ounces well-trimmed pork tenderloin, cut into ½-inch chunks

1 tablespoon olive oil

1 onion, cut into ½-inch chunks

1 red bell pepper, cut into ½-inch pieces

1½ cups peeled baby carrots

1⅔ cups reduced-sodium chicken broth, defatted

½ teaspoon dried oregano

1 banana, finely diced

1 tablespoon plus 2 teaspoons creamy peanut butter

1 cup frozen peas

1½ cups couscous

2½ cups boiling water

1. On a sheet of waxed paper, combine the flour, ¼ teaspoon of the salt, and ¼ teaspoon of the black pepper. Dredge the pork in the flour mixture, shaking off the excess. In a large nonstick skillet, heat 2 teaspoons of the oil until hot but not smoking over medium heat. Add the pork and cook, stirring frequently, until browned, about 4 minutes. With a slotted spoon, transfer the pork to a plate.

2. Add the remaining 1 teaspoon oil to the skillet and heat until hot but not smoking over medium heat. Add the onion, bell pepper, and carrots and cook, stirring frequently, until the onion is lightly browned, about 5 minutes. Stir in the broth, oregano, the remaining ½ teaspoon salt, and remaining ¼ teaspoon black pepper. Bring to a boil, reduce to a simmer, cover, and cook until the vegetables are crisp-tender, about 10 minutes. Stir in the banana, peanut butter, and peas; return the pork to the pan and cook until the pork is cooked through but still juicy, about 4 minutes.

3. Meanwhile, in a medium bowl, combine the couscous and boiling water. Stir well, cover, and let stand until the couscous has softened, about 5 minutes. Fluff the couscous with a fork and divide among 4 bowls. Spoon the stew over the couscous and serve.

Helpful hint: You can cut up the onion and bell pepper in advance and refrigerate them until needed; but dice the banana just before using.

FAT: 10G/17%
CALORIES: 529
SATURATED FAT: 2G
CARBOHYDRATE: 78G
PROTEIN: 31G
CHOLESTEROL: 46MG
SODIUM: 777MG

A creative interpretation of several African dishes, this unusual stew will brighten appetites jaded by everyday fare. The sautéed pork chunks, combined with onion, bell pepper, carrots, and peas, are familiar enough; but the exotic-tasting sauce is made with peanut butter and diced banana. The stew is served over couscous, the tiny North African pasta.

THREE-ALARM PORK AND BEEF CHILI

SERVES: 4
WORKING TIME: 25 MINUTES
TOTAL TIME: 50 MINUTES

*W*atch out—"three-alarm" means hot! But you can cut down on the cayenne, chili powder, and jalapeños if you prefer a tamer chili.

1 cup long-grain rice

1 teaspoon salt

2 tablespoons flour

2 teaspoons chili powder

1 teaspoon dried oregano

1 teaspoon ground cumin

¼ teaspoon cayenne pepper

6 ounces well-trimmed pork tenderloin, cut into ½-inch chunks

4 ounces well-trimmed top round of beef, cut into ½-inch chunks

1 tablespoon olive oil

1 onion, finely chopped

5 cloves garlic, minced

2 green bell peppers, cut into ½-inch squares

2 pickled jalapeños, finely chopped

1 cup dry red wine

14½-ounce can no-salt-added stewed tomatoes, chopped with their juices

19-ounce can pinto beans, rinsed and drained

1. In a medium saucepan, bring 2¼ cups of water to a boil. Add the rice and ¼ teaspoon of the salt, reduce to a simmer, cover, and cook until the rice is tender, about 17 minutes.

2. Meanwhile, on a sheet of waxed paper, combine the flour, chili powder, oregano, cumin, and cayenne. Dredge the pork and beef in the seasoned flour, shaking off and reserving the excess. In a large nonstick saucepan or Dutch oven, heat 2 teaspoons of the oil until hot but not smoking over medium heat. Add the meat and cook, stirring frequently, until browned, about 4 minutes. With a slotted spoon, transfer the meat to a plate.

3. Add the remaining 1 teaspoon oil to the pan. Add the onion and garlic and cook, stirring frequently, until the onion is tender, about 7 minutes. Add the bell peppers and jalapeños and cook, stirring frequently, until the bell peppers are tender, about 5 minutes. Sprinkle the reserved flour mixture over, stirring to coat. Return the meat to the pan, add the wine, increase the heat to high, and cook until evaporated, about 3 minutes. Add the tomatoes, beans, the remaining ¾ teaspoon salt, and ½ cup of water. Reduce to a simmer, cover, and cook until the meat is tender and the sauce is richly flavored, about 20 minutes.

4. Divide the rice among 4 bowls, spoon the chili over, and serve.

FAT: 7G/14%
CALORIES: 446
SATURATED FAT: 1.4G
CARBOHYDRATE: 69G
PROTEIN: 27G
CHOLESTEROL: 44MG
SODIUM: 953MG

Pork Burgoo

SERVES: 4
WORKING TIME: 30 MINUTES
TOTAL TIME: 40 MINUTES

1 pound all-purpose potatoes, peeled and cut into ½-inch chunks

2 tablespoons flour

1 teaspoon salt

¾ pound well-trimmed pork tenderloin, cut into ½-inch chunks

1 tablespoon olive oil

1 onion, cut into ½-inch cubes

1½ cups peeled baby carrots

4 cups green cabbage, cut into ½-inch chunks

14½-ounce can no-salt-added stewed tomatoes, chopped with their juices

1 cup reduced-sodium chicken broth, defatted

1½ teaspoons Worcestershire sauce

½ teaspoon dried thyme

½ teaspoon freshly ground black pepper

1½ cups frozen corn kernels

1. In a medium pot of boiling water, cook the potatoes for 7 minutes to blanch. Drain.

2. Meanwhile, on a sheet of waxed paper, combine the flour and ¼ teaspoon of the salt. Dredge the pork in the flour mixture, shaking off and reserving the excess. In a large nonstick skillet or Dutch oven, heat the oil until hot but not smoking over medium heat. Add the pork and cook, stirring frequently, until browned, about 4 minutes. With a slotted spoon, transfer the pork to a plate.

3. Add the onion and carrots to the pan and cook, stirring frequently, until the onion is tender, about 7 minutes. Add the cabbage and cook, stirring, until the cabbage is wilted, about 7 minutes. Return the pork to the pan, sprinkle with the reserved flour mixture, stirring to coat. Add the tomatoes, potatoes, broth, Worcestershire sauce, thyme, the remaining ¾ teaspoon salt, and the pepper and bring to a boil. Reduce to a simmer, cover, and cook until the meat and vegetables are tender, about 8 minutes. Stir in the corn and cook just until heated through, about 2 minutes.

Helpful hint: For a variation, you can make this stew with a lean cut of lamb, such as shank, instead of the pork, if you like.

FAT: 7G/18%
CALORIES: 352
SATURATED FAT: 1.6G
CARBOHYDRATE: 50G
PROTEIN: 25G
CHOLESTEROL: 55MG
SODIUM: 807MG

Pork takes the place of the small game (such as rabbit) traditionally used in this old-time Southern stew.

GREEK BEEF STEW

SERVES: 4
WORKING TIME: 35 MINUTES
TOTAL TIME: 35 MINUTES

A true Greek stifado is baked in a slow oven for two to three hours, but our stew simmers on the stove in much less time. We've kept the traditional Greek flavors of lemon, oregano, olive oil, and garlic, but added potatoes, bell pepper, and green beans to a dish that's usually made with onions alone. Bring the stew to the table in a rustic ceramic tureen; serve with warm pita bread.

1 pound all-purpose potatoes, peeled and cut into ¼-inch dice

½ pound green beans, halved crosswise

2 tablespoons flour

1 teaspoon salt

¼ teaspoon freshly ground black pepper

10 ounces well-trimmed beef sirloin, cut into ½-inch chunks

1 tablespoon olive oil

1 onion, finely chopped

3 cloves garlic, minced

1 green bell pepper, cut into ½-inch squares

1 teaspoon dried oregano

1 teaspoon paprika

14½-ounce can no-salt-added stewed tomatoes, chopped with their juices

Two 8-ounce cans no-salt-added tomato sauce

1 teaspoon grated lemon zest

⅓ cup snipped fresh dill

1. In a large pot of boiling water, cook the potatoes until tender, about 5 minutes. Add the green beans for the last 3 minutes of cooking time. Drain.

2. Meanwhile, on a sheet of waxed paper, combine the flour, ¼ teaspoon of the salt, and the black pepper. Dredge the beef in the flour mixture, shaking off the excess. In a large nonstick skillet or Dutch oven, heat 2 teaspoons of the oil until hot but not smoking over medium heat. Add the beef and cook, stirring frequently, until browned, about 4 minutes. With a slotted spoon, transfer the beef to a plate.

3. Add the remaining 1 teaspoon oil to the skillet and heat until hot but not smoking. Add the onion and garlic and cook, stirring frequently, until the onion is softened, about 7 minutes. Add the bell pepper, oregano, and paprika and cook, stirring frequently, until the bell pepper is crisp-tender, about 4 minutes.

4. Stir the tomatoes, tomato sauce, lemon zest, and the remaining ¾ teaspoon salt into the pan and bring to a boil. Reduce to a simmer, return the beef to the pan along with the dill, potatoes, and green beans and cook until the beef is just cooked through and the potatoes and green beans are hot, about 3 minutes.

Helpful hint: If fresh dill is not available, substitute chopped fresh parsley.

FAT: 8G/23%
CALORIES: 318
SATURATED FAT: 1.6G
CARBOHYDRATE: 44G
PROTEIN: 22G
CHOLESTEROL: 43MG
SODIUM: 647MG

GARLIC-CHILI PORK STEW

SERVES: 4
WORKING TIME: 40 MINUTES
TOTAL TIME: 40 MINUTES

With ginger and lime juice as seasonings, this dish has a definite Asian air. But there are also sweet potatoes, chili sauce, and olive oil in the recipe, so it's hardly a classic dish. The sweetly spicy pork and vegetables are served over steamed rice, and all you need for a complete meal is some fresh fruit for dessert. If necessary, you can substitute fresh or frozen snow peas for the sugar snaps.

3 tablespoons fresh lime juice

4 cloves garlic, minced

1 teaspoon chili powder

½ teaspoon freshly ground black pepper

¾ pound well-trimmed pork tenderloin, cut into ½-inch chunks

1 cup long-grain rice

¾ teaspoon salt

1 pound sweet potatoes, peeled and cut into ½-inch chunks

½ pound sugar snap peas, strings removed

3 tablespoons flour

1 tablespoon olive oil

3 scallions, thinly sliced

2 tablespoons finely chopped fresh ginger

1¼ cups reduced-sodium chicken broth, defatted

¼ cup chili sauce

2 teaspoons firmly packed light brown sugar

1. In a medium bowl, combine the lime juice, garlic, chili powder, and pepper. Add the pork, stirring to coat; set aside for 10 minutes to marinate. In a medium saucepan, bring 2¼ cups of water to a boil. Add the rice and ¼ teaspoon of the salt, reduce to a simmer, cover, and cook until the rice is tender, about 17 minutes. In a large pot of boiling water, cook the sweet potatoes until tender, about 7 minutes. Add the sugar snap peas during the last 1 minute of cooking time. Drain.

2. Meanwhile, reserving the marinade, remove the pork and pat dry with paper towels. Sprinkle the flour over the pork, patting it in. In a large nonstick skillet, heat the oil until hot but not smoking over medium heat. Add the pork and cook, stirring frequently, until browned on all sides, about 4 minutes. Transfer the pork to a plate.

3. Add the scallions and ginger to the pan and cook until the scallions are softened, about 3 minutes. Add the broth and the reserved marinade and cook until the garlic is softened, about 4 minutes. Stir in the chili sauce, brown sugar, and the remaining ½ teaspoon salt and bring to a boil. Reduce to a simmer and cook until slightly thickened, about 4 minutes. Return the pork to the pan along with the sweet potatoes and sugar snap peas and cook until the pork is cooked through and the vegetables are hot, about 3 minutes. Divide the rice among 4 bowls, spoon the stew over, and serve.

FAT: 7G/13%
CALORIES: 478
SATURATED FAT: 1.6G
CARBOHYDRATE: 76G
PROTEIN: 26G
CHOLESTEROL: 55MG
SODIUM: 881MG

Onions are usually thought of as pungent or even bitter-tasting, but when slowly sautéed (with a sprinkling of sugar to help them along), they caramelize, developing a rich sweetness that complements pork beautifully. To balance the sweetness, the pan is deglazed here with wine vinegar. Use any medium tube-shaped pasta, such as ziti, penne, or rigatoni.

PORK STEW WITH PASTA AND CARAMELIZED ONIONS

SERVES: 4
WORKING TIME: 30 MINUTES
TOTAL TIME: 45 MINUTES

8 ounces pasta tubes, such as ziti

4 teaspoons olive oil

1½ cups frozen or fresh pearl onions (see tip)

1½ cups peeled baby carrots

6 scallions, cut into 1-inch lengths

1 tablespoon sugar

2 tablespoons flour

¾ teaspoon salt

½ teaspoon freshly ground black pepper

¾ pound well-trimmed pork tenderloin, cut into ½-inch chunks

¼ cup red wine vinegar

1½ cups reduced-sodium chicken broth, defatted

1 tablespoon no-salt-added tomato paste

½ teaspoon dried sage

½ teaspoon dried oregano

1. In a large pot of boiling water, cook the pasta until just tender. Drain well.

2. Meanwhile, in a large nonstick skillet, heat 2 teaspoons of the oil until hot but not smoking over medium heat. Add the pearl onions, carrots, scallions, and sugar and cook, shaking the pan frequently, until the onions are golden brown, about 12 minutes.

3. On a sheet of waxed paper, combine the flour, ¼ teaspoon of the salt, and ¼ teaspoon of the pepper. Dredge the pork in the flour mixture, shaking off the excess. In a separate nonstick skillet, heat the remaining 2 teaspoons oil until hot but not smoking over medium heat. Add the pork and cook, stirring frequently, until golden brown, about 4 minutes. Transfer the pork to the pan with the onions.

4. Add the vinegar to the pan the pork was cooked in, scraping up any browned bits that cling to the pan. Pour the vinegar mixture into the pan with the onions and pork and stir in the broth, tomato paste, sage, oregano, the remaining ½ teaspoon salt, and remaining ¼ teaspoon pepper. Bring to a boil, reduce to a simmer, cover, and cook until the pork and vegetables are tender, about 15 minutes. Divide the pasta among 4 bowls, spoon the pork over, and serve.

FAT: 9G/18%
CALORIES: 441
SATURATED FAT: 1.7G
CARBOHYDRATE: 62G
PROTEIN: 28G
CHOLESTEROL: 55MG
SODIUM: 696MG

TIP

If you prefer to use fresh pearl onions, you'll need to blanch and peel them. Blanch the whole onions in a large pot of boiling water for 1-2 minutes; drain, cool briefly under cold water, and then peel them.

TEX-MEX BEEF STEW

SERVES: 4
WORKING TIME: 20 MINUTES
TOTAL TIME: 30 MINUTES

1 cup long-grain rice

¾ teaspoon salt

2 tablespoons flour

½ teaspoon freshly ground black pepper

10 ounces well-trimmed beef sirloin, cut into ½-inch chunks

2 teaspoons olive oil

6 scallions, cut into 1-inch lengths

3 cloves garlic, minced

2 cups no-salt-added canned tomatoes, chopped with their juices

4½-ounce can chopped mild green chilies, drained

2 tablespoons fresh lime juice

1½ cups frozen corn kernels

½ cup chopped fresh cilantro or basil

1. In a medium saucepan, bring 2¼ cups of water to a boil. Add the rice and ¼ teaspoon of the salt, reduce to a simmer, cover, and cook until the rice is tender, about 17 minutes.

2. Meanwhile, on a sheet of waxed paper, combine the flour, ¼ teaspoon of the salt, and the pepper. Dredge the beef in the flour mixture, shaking off the excess.

3. In a large nonstick skillet or Dutch oven, heat the oil until hot but not smoking over medium heat. Add the beef and cook, stirring frequently, until browned, about 4 minutes. Stir in the scallions and garlic and cook until the scallions are softened, about 3 minutes. Add the tomatoes, chilies, lime juice, the remaining ¼ teaspoon salt, and ¼ cup of water. Bring to a boil, reduce to a simmer, cover, and cook until the beef is just cooked through and the sauce is slightly thickened, about 10 minutes.

4. Stir the corn and cilantro into the pan and cook just until the corn is heated through, about 2 minutes. Divide the rice evenly among 4 plates, spoon the stew alongside, and serve.

Helpful hint: For an extra touch of flavor and color, sprinkle the rice with 1 teaspoon chopped fresh herbs—cilantro, basil, or parsley.

FAT: 7G/16%
CALORIES: 395
SATURATED FAT: 1.6G
CARBOHYDRATE: 63G
PROTEIN: 23G
CHOLESTEROL: 43MG
SODIUM: 672MG

Many of the dishes Texas is famous for begin with beef—the pride of the state—and the Mexican flavorings that Texans have come to love. This beef stew makes the most of both: Sirloin chunks, corn kernels, and scallions get the Tex-Mex treatment with tomatoes, garlic, green chilies, lime juice, and the herby kick of fresh cilantro. Fresh biscuits or rolls are a fine accompaniment.

BRAISED PORK WITH TOMATOES AND ROSEMARY

SERVES: 4
WORKING TIME: 20 MINUTES
TOTAL TIME: 25 MINUTES

An herb with a bold personality, rosemary announces its presence with a compelling fragrance and a robust flavor. So it's best matched with foods that can also hold their own—in this case, thick cutlets of pork loin, tomatoes, red wine, garlic, and mushrooms. The pasta (you could substitute rice for a change) serves as a foil for all that flavor.

8 ounces orzo pasta

2 tablespoons flour

¾ teaspoon salt

½ teaspoon freshly ground black pepper

10 ounces well-trimmed center-cut pork loin, cut into 4 slices

1 tablespoon olive oil

3 cloves garlic, slivered

¼ pound mushrooms, thickly sliced

⅔ cup dry red wine

2 cups no-salt-added canned tomatoes, chopped with their juices

½ teaspoon dried rosemary, crumbled

⅛ teaspoon red pepper flakes

1 teaspoon cornstarch mixed with 1 tablespoon water

¼ cup chopped fresh parsley

1. In a large pot of boiling water, cook the pasta until just tender. Drain well.

2. Meanwhile, on a sheet of waxed paper, combine the flour, ¼ teaspoon of the salt, and the black pepper. Dredge the pork in the flour mixture, shaking off the excess. In a large nonstick skillet, heat the oil until hot but not smoking over high heat. Add the pork and cook, stirring frequently, until lightly browned, about 1 minute per side. Transfer the pork to a plate.

3. Add the garlic to the skillet and cook, stirring frequently, until softened, about 3 minutes. Add the mushrooms and cook, stirring frequently, until tender, about 4 minutes. Add the wine, increase the heat to high, and cook until the liquid has reduced by half, about 4 minutes.

4. Stir the tomatoes, rosemary, red pepper flakes, and the remaining ½ teaspoon salt into the pan. Bring to a boil, reduce to a simmer, and return the pork to the pan. Cook until the pork is just cooked through and the sauce is flavorful, about 2 minutes. Add the cornstarch mixture and cook, stirring, until slightly thickened, about 1 minute. Stir in the parsley. Divide the pasta among 4 bowls, spoon the pork mixture alongside, and serve.

Helpful hint: Chilling the pork in the freezer will make it easier to slice.

FAT: 8G/18%
CALORIES: 396
SATURATED FAT: 1.9G
CARBOHYDRATE: 54G
PROTEIN: 25G
CHOLESTEROL: 45MG
SODIUM: 483MG

Braised Beef with Tarragon

SERVES: 4
WORKING TIME: 20 MINUTES
TOTAL TIME: 30 MINUTES

There's something wonderful about the combination of mushrooms and tarragon. Here, two types of mushrooms double the impact.

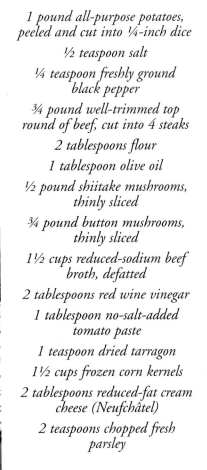

1 pound all-purpose potatoes, peeled and cut into ¼-inch dice

½ teaspoon salt

¼ teaspoon freshly ground black pepper

¾ pound well-trimmed top round of beef, cut into 4 steaks

2 tablespoons flour

1 tablespoon olive oil

½ pound shiitake mushrooms, thinly sliced

¾ pound button mushrooms, thinly sliced

1½ cups reduced-sodium beef broth, defatted

2 tablespoons red wine vinegar

1 tablespoon no-salt-added tomato paste

1 teaspoon dried tarragon

1½ cups frozen corn kernels

2 tablespoons reduced-fat cream cheese (Neufchâtel)

2 teaspoons chopped fresh parsley

1. In a large pot of boiling water, cook the potatoes until firm-tender, about 5 minutes. Drain.

2. Meanwhile, sprinkle the salt and pepper over the beef, rubbing it in. Rub the flour into the beef. In a large nonstick skillet, heat 2 teaspoons of the oil until hot but not smoking over medium heat. Add the beef and cook until browned, about 2 minutes per side. Transfer the beef to a plate.

3. Add the remaining 1 teaspoon oil to the pan and heat until hot but not smoking. Add the shiitake and button mushrooms, stirring to coat. Add ½ cup of the broth, cover, and cook until the mushrooms are tender, about 4 minutes. Stir in the remaining 1 cup broth, the vinegar, tomato paste, and tarragon and bring to a boil. Reduce to a simmer, return the beef to the pan, and add the corn and potatoes. Cook until the beef, corn, and potatoes are heated through, about 3 minutes.

4. With a slotted spoon, transfer the beef to 4 bowls. Stir the cream cheese and parsley into the skillet, bring to a boil, and stir until the cream cheese is melted. Spoon the sauce over the beef and serve.

Helpful hint: If you can't find shiitakes, simply use an additional ½ pound of button mushrooms.

FAT: 9G/24%
CALORIES: 339
SATURATED FAT: 2.6G
CARBOHYDRATE: 40G
PROTEIN: 29G
CHOLESTEROL: 54MG
SODIUM: 595MG

Beef Stew with Apples and Ginger

SERVES: 4
WORKING TIME: 25 MINUTES
TOTAL TIME: 40 MINUTES

8 ounces wide egg noodles

2 tablespoons flour

¾ teaspoon salt

½ teaspoon freshly ground black pepper

¼ teaspoon ground ginger

10 ounces well-trimmed beef sirloin, cut into ½-inch chunks

1 tablespoon olive oil

2 onions, cut into ½-inch chunks

3 cloves garlic, minced

2 sweet apples, such as McIntosh, Cortland, or Delicious, peeled, cored, and cut into ½-inch chunks

2 cups reduced-sodium chicken broth, defatted

2 ounces gingersnap cookies, crumbled

3 tablespoons cider vinegar

1 teaspoon chopped fresh parsley (optional)

1. In a large pot of boiling water, cook the noodles until just tender. Drain well.

2. Meanwhile, on a sheet of waxed paper, combine the flour, ¼ teaspoon of the salt, ¼ teaspoon of the pepper, and the ginger. Dredge the beef in the flour mixture, shaking off the excess. In a large nonstick skillet or Dutch oven, heat the oil until hot but not smoking over medium heat. Add the beef and cook, stirring frequently, until browned, about 4 minutes. With a slotted spoon, transfer the beef to a plate.

3. Add the onions and garlic to the pan and cook, stirring frequently, until the onions are tender, about 7 minutes. Add the apples and cook, stirring frequently, until lightly golden, about 3 minutes. Add the broth, gingersnaps, vinegar, the remaining ½ teaspoon salt, remaining ¼ teaspoon pepper, and ½ cup of water and bring to a boil.

4. Return the beef to the pan, reduce to a simmer, cover, and cook until the beef is tender, about 15 minutes. Toss the stew with the noodles, divide among 4 plates, sprinkle the parsley over, and serve.

Helpful hint: For a change, serve the stew over rice or mashed potatoes.

FAT: 11G/20%
CALORIES: 493
SATURATED FAT: 2.3G
CARBOHYDRATE: 73G
PROTEIN: 27G
CHOLESTEROL: 97MG
SODIUM: 841MG

Here's something new: a beef stew with the autumnal spiciness of baked apples. It's tossed with wide noodles.

VINEYARD PORK STEW

SERVES: 4
WORKING TIME: 25 MINUTES
TOTAL TIME: 40 MINUTES

The name of this recipe has a triple meaning: The dish is made with plump grapes, white wine, and balsamic vinegar—all products of the vineyard. The wine is cooked down to fortify the sauce, and its fragrance and flavor suffuse the potatoes and pork. Balance the richness by serving a crisp, lightly dressed salad with the stew.

1 pound all-purpose potatoes, peeled and cut into ½-inch chunks

1 teaspoon paprika

¾ pound well-trimmed pork tenderloin, cut into ½-inch chunks

2 tablespoons flour

¾ teaspoon salt

½ teaspoon freshly ground black pepper

2½ teaspoons olive oil

1 red onion, finely chopped

3 cloves garlic, minced

2 carrots, thinly sliced

⅔ cup dry white wine

1½ cups reduced-sodium chicken broth, defatted

2 tablespoons balsamic vinegar

2 cups green or red seedless grapes

¼ cup chopped fresh parsley

1. In a large pot of boiling water, cook the potatoes for 7 minutes to blanch. Drain.

2. Meanwhile, rub the paprika into the pork. On a sheet of waxed paper, combine the flour, ¼ teaspoon of the salt, and the pepper. Dredge the pork in the flour mixture, shaking off and reserving the excess. In a large nonstick skillet or Dutch oven, heat the oil until hot but not smoking over medium heat. Add the pork and cook, stirring frequently, until lightly browned, about 4 minutes. With a slotted spoon, transfer the pork to a plate.

3. Add the onion and garlic to the skillet and cook, stirring frequently, until the onion is tender, about 5 minutes. Add the carrots and cook, stirring frequently, until tender, about 5 minutes. Return the pork to the pan and sprinkle with the reserved flour mixture. Add the wine, increase the heat to high, and cook until the wine has evaporated by half, about 3 minutes.

4. Add the broth, vinegar, the remaining ½ teaspoon salt, and the potatoes to the pan. Reduce to a simmer, cover, and cook until the pork is tender and the potatoes have cooked through, about 15 minutes. Add the grapes and cook until heated through, about 2 minutes. Stir in the parsley, divide among 4 bowls, and serve.

FAT: 7G/20%
CALORIES: 313
SATURATED FAT: 1.6G
CARBOHYDRATE: 42G
PROTEIN: 23G
CHOLESTEROL: 55MG
SODIUM: 693MG

Hidden inside these Italian-style involtini (rolled cutlets) is a delicious bread-and-Parmesan filling and a hint of mustard. The sauce is bright with cubes of carrot and zucchini, along with the luxurious surprise of velvety pine nuts. To do the dish justice, be sure to use a good-quality Parmesan (preferably imported), freshly grated.

Braised Pork with Pine Nuts and Parmesan

Serves: 4
Working time: 20 minutes
Total time: 30 minutes

8 ounces orzo pasta

½ pound well-trimmed pork loin, cut into 8 slices and pounded (see page 8) ⅛ inch thick

4 teaspoons Dijon mustard

½ teaspoon salt

2 slices (2 ounces total) firm-textured white bread, finely crumbled

¼ cup grated Parmesan cheese

2 tablespoons flour

2 teaspoons olive oil

2 carrots, finely diced

1 zucchini, finely diced

1¼ cups reduced-sodium chicken broth, defatted

¾ teaspoon grated lemon zest

2 tablespoon fresh lemon juice

⅓ cup chopped fresh mint

½ teaspoon dried rosemary, crumbled

¼ teaspoon freshly ground black pepper

2 tablespoons pine nuts

1. In a large pot of boiling water, cook the pasta until just tender. Drain well.

2. Meanwhile, brush the tops of the pork slices with the mustard. Sprinkle ¼ teaspoon of the salt over. Sprinkle the bread crumbs and Parmesan over, lightly pressing down (see tip; top photo). Roll up the pork from one short end and secure with toothpicks (bottom photo).

3. Dredge the pork rolls in the flour, shaking off and reserving the excess. In a large nonstick skillet, heat the oil until hot but not smoking over medium heat. Cook the pork, turning frequently, until lightly browned, about 3 minutes. Transfer the pork rolls to a plate. Add the carrots and zucchini to the skillet. Stir in 1 cup of the broth, the lemon zest, lemon juice, mint, rosemary, pepper, and the remaining ¼ teaspoon salt. Bring to a boil, reduce to a simmer, and return the pork rolls to the pan. Cover, and cook until the pork is tender and the sauce is flavorful, about 10 minutes.

4. In a small bowl, combine the remaining ¼ cup broth and the reserved flour mixture. Stir the broth mixture into the skillet along with the pine nuts and cook, stirring, until the sauce is slightly thickened, about 2 minutes. Divide the pasta among 4 plates. Remove the toothpicks from the pork rolls and serve the pork rolls and vegetable mixture alongside the pasta.

Fat: 11g/22%
Calories: 444
Saturated Fat: 3g
Carbohydrate: 59g
Protein: 26g
Cholesterol: 38mg
Sodium: 786mg

TIP

After brushing the tops of the pork slices with mustard and seasoning them with salt, press the crumbs and Parmesan into the surface of the meat. Starting at one short end, roll up the pork with the breading inside. Secure the rolls with toothpicks.

PROVENÇAL PORK STEW

SERVES: 4
WORKING TIME: 25 MINUTES
TOTAL TIME: 35 MINUTES

8 ounces penne pasta

2 tablespoons flour

¾ teaspoon salt

10 ounces well-trimmed pork tenderloin, cut into ½-inch chunks

1 tablespoon olive oil

1 small eggplant (¾ pound), peeled and cut into ½-inch cubes

2 red bell peppers, cut into ½-inch squares

1 red onion, coarsely chopped

3 cloves garlic, minced

2¼ cups no-salt-added canned tomatoes, chopped with their juices

¼ cup chopped fresh basil

¾ teaspoon dried tarragon

¼ cup slivered Calamata olives

1 tablespoon capers, rinsed and drained

1 tablespoon balsamic vinegar

1 teaspoon cornstarch mixed with 1 tablespoon water

1. In a large pot of boiling water, cook the pasta until just tender. Drain well.

2. Meanwhile, on a sheet of waxed paper, combine the flour and ¼ teaspoon of the salt. Dredge the pork in the flour mixture, shaking off the excess. In a large nonstick skillet, heat 2 teaspoons of the oil until hot but not smoking over medium heat. Add the pork and cook, stirring frequently, until lightly browned, about 4 minutes. With a slotted spoon, transfer the pork to a plate.

3. Add the remaining 1 teaspoon oil to the pan and heat until hot but not smoking. Add the eggplant, bell peppers, onion, and garlic and cook, stirring to coat. Add ½ cup of water, cover, and cook until the vegetables are crisp-tender, about 5 minutes.

4. Stir the tomatoes, basil, tarragon, olives, capers, vinegar, and the remaining ½ teaspoon salt into the skillet. Bring to a boil, reduce to a simmer, return the pork to the pan, cover, and cook until the pork is just cooked through and the sauce is flavorful, about 6 minutes. Stir in the cornstarch mixture and cook, stirring, until slightly thickened, about 1 minute. Transfer the pasta to a platter or bowl, spoon the pork mixture over, and serve.

Helpful hint: Another type of olive may be substituted for Calamatas. Brine-cured Niçoise olives would be particularly appropriate.

FAT: 10G/20%
CALORIES: 447
SATURATED FAT: 1.8G
CARBOHYDRATE: 65G
PROTEIN: 26G
CHOLESTEROL: 46MG
SODIUM: 725MG

The presence of eggplant, bell peppers, tomatoes, and olives, as well as the generous use of herbs, mark this as a Provençal dish. When simmered together, these ingredients form an earthy setting for tender cubes of pork. Provence borders on Italy, so it's not surprising that pasta is quite popular in this beautiful corner of France.

INDIAN-STYLE BRAISED PORK

SERVES: 4
WORKING TIME: 30 MINUTES
TOTAL TIME: 35 MINUTES

A heady blend of cumin, coriander, turmeric, and cayenne serves as both a spice rub and a sauce seasoning in this Indian-inspired dish. The "custom-made" spice mixture honors the Indian culinary tradition of devising seasonings to suit specific foods, rather than simply adding curry powder to every dish. Turmeric not only flavors the dish, it also gives it a rich, golden color.

1 cup long-grain rice
¾ teaspoon salt
¾ teaspoon ground cumin
¾ teaspoon ground coriander
¾ teaspoon ground ginger
½ teaspoon turmeric
¼ teaspoon cayenne pepper
10 ounces well-trimmed pork loin, cut into 4 slices and pounded (see page 8) ½ inch thick
3 tablespoons flour
1 tablespoon olive oil
1 onion, finely chopped
2 cloves garlic, minced
8-ounce can no-salt-added tomato sauce
¼ cup golden raisins
1 cup frozen peas
½ cup plain nonfat yogurt
2 tablespoons slivered almonds

1. In a medium saucepan, bring 2¼ cups of water to a boil. Add the rice and ¼ teaspoon of the salt, reduce to a simmer, cover, and cook until the rice is tender, about 17 minutes.

2. Meanwhile, in a small bowl, combine the cumin, coriander, ginger, turmeric, and cayenne. Rub 1½ teaspoons of the spice mixture into the pork. Reserve the remainder. Dredge the pork in 2 tablespoons of the flour, shaking off the excess.

3. In a large nonstick skillet, heat the oil until hot but not smoking over medium heat. Add the pork and cook until lightly browned, about 1 minute per side. Transfer the pork to a plate. Add the onion and garlic to the pan and cook, stirring frequently, until the onion is softened, about 4 minutes. Add the tomato sauce, raisins, peas, the reserved spice mixture, the remaining ½ teaspoon salt, and ½ cup of water. Bring to a boil, reduce to a simmer, and return the pork to the pan. Cover and cook until the pork is just cooked through, about 4 minutes.

4. With a slotted spoon, transfer the pork to a plate. In a small bowl, combine the remaining 1 tablespoon flour and the yogurt. Add the yogurt mixture to the pan along with the almonds and cook, stirring, until slightly thickened and no floury taste remains, about 2 minutes. Divide the vegetable-raisin sauce among 4 plates, top with the pork, spoon the rice alongside, and serve.

FAT: 11G/22%
CALORIES: 459
SATURATED FAT: 2.2G
CARBOHYDRATE: 66G
PROTEIN: 25G
CHOLESTEROL: 42MG
SODIUM: 529MG

BRAISED SOY SAUCE BEEF AND VEGETABLES

SERVES: 4
WORKING TIME: 20 MINUTES
TOTAL TIME: 1 HOUR

*R*ich
with Chinese flavors,
this dish is braised, not
stir-fried. The soy
sauce, sherry, and
ginger are enlivened
with cinnamon.

¼ cup reduced-sodium soy sauce

¼ cup sherry

2 tablespoons firmly packed dark brown sugar

3 tablespoons chopped fresh ginger

3 scallions, thinly sliced

2 cloves garlic, minced

¼ teaspoon cinnamon

¾ pound well-trimmed top round of beef, in one piece

¼ pound fresh shiitake or button mushrooms, thinly sliced

2 carrots, cut into 2 x ¼-inch julienne strips

1 red bell pepper, cut into 2 x ¼-inch strips

1 green bell pepper, cut into 2 x ¼-inch strips

1 cup long-grain rice

¼ teaspoon salt

1¾ teaspoons cornstarch mixed with 1 tablespoon water

1. In a medium saucepan, combine the soy sauce, sherry, brown sugar, ginger, scallions, garlic, cinnamon, and 1 cup of water over medium heat. Bring to a boil, reduce to a simmer, cover, and cook for 5 minutes to blend the flavors. Add the beef, cover, and simmer for 20 minutes. Add the mushrooms, carrots, and bell peppers; cover and simmer until the beef is tender, about 20 minutes.

2. Meanwhile, in a medium saucepan, bring 2¼ cups of water to a boil. Add the rice and salt, reduce to a simmer, cover, and cook until the rice is tender, about 17 minutes.

3. Remove the beef from the pan and set aside. Bring the mixture in the pan to a boil, stir in the cornstarch mixture, and cook, stirring, until slightly thickened, about 1 minute. Thinly slice the beef.

4. Divide the rice among 4 plates. Top with the slices of beef, spoon the sauce over, and serve.

Helpful hint: You can substitute dry vermouth, brandy, dry white wine, or bourbon for the sherry if you like.

FAT: 3G/7%
CALORIES: 365
SATURATED FAT: 1.1G
CARBOHYDRATE: 58G
PROTEIN: 25G
CHOLESTEROL: 49MG
SODIUM: 802MG

STIR-FRIES & SAUTÉS

2

Sautéed Pork with Eggplant-Tomato Sauce

Serves: 4
Working time: 25 minutes
Total time: 35 minutes

You don't need to cook a vegetable side dish for these sautéed pork cutlets, because the sauce includes eggplant, celery, and tomatoes. Pine nuts add a touch of richness, while a handful of parsley gives the sauce a fresh flavor. Pasta shells, served with the pork, catch the savory sauce. Begin the meal with a crisp salad, or offer a salad as an accompaniment to the entrée.

8 ounces small pasta shells
2 tablespoons flour
¾ teaspoon salt
½ teaspoon freshly ground black pepper
¾ pound well-trimmed pork tenderloin, cut into 8 slices and pounded (see page 8) ½ inch thick
1 tablespoon olive oil
2 ribs celery, halved lengthwise and thinly sliced
1 small eggplant (10 ounces), unpeeled and cut into ½-inch cubes
1 cup reduced-sodium chicken broth, defatted
14½-ounce can no-salt-added stewed tomatoes, chopped with their juices
2 tablespoons no-salt-added tomato paste
2 tablespoons capers, rinsed and drained
1 teaspoon chili powder
1 tablespoon pine nuts
¼ cup chopped fresh parsley

1. In a large pot of boiling water, cook the pasta until just tender. Drain well.

2. Meanwhile, on a sheet of waxed paper, combine the flour, ¼ teaspoon of the salt, and ¼ teaspoon of the pepper. Dredge the pork in the flour mixture, shaking off the excess. In a large nonstick skillet, heat 2 teaspoons of the oil until hot but not smoking over medium-high heat. Add the pork and cook until lightly browned, about 1 minute per side. Transfer the pork to a plate.

3. Add the remaining 1 teaspoon oil to the skillet and heat until hot but not smoking. Reduce the heat to medium, add the celery and eggplant and cook, stirring frequently, until coated, about 1 minute. Add ½ cup of the broth, cover, and cook until the eggplant is tender, about 5 minutes. Add the tomatoes and their juices, the tomato paste, capers, chili powder, the remaining ½ cup broth, remaining ½ teaspoon salt, and remaining ¼ teaspoon pepper. Bring to a boil, reduce to a simmer, and cook until slightly thickened and richly flavored, about 5 minutes.

4. Return the pork to the pan, add the pine nuts and parsley, and cook just until the pork is cooked through, about 2 minutes. Divide the pasta among 4 plates, spoon the pork and sauce alongside, and serve.

Fat: 9g/19%
Calories: 433
Saturated Fat: 1.8g
Carbohydrate: 60g
Protein: 29g
Cholesterol: 55mg
Sodium: 840mg

STIR-FRIED KOREAN-STYLE BEEF

SERVES: 4
WORKING TIME: 30 MINUTES
TOTAL TIME: 30 MINUTES

1 cup long-grain rice

½ teaspoon salt

4 teaspoons cornstarch

½ cup reduced-sodium chicken broth, defatted

3 tablespoons reduced-sodium soy sauce

2 tablespoons rice vinegar

2 teaspoons sesame seeds

1 teaspoon dark Oriental sesame oil

½ teaspoon sugar

½ pound well-trimmed beef sirloin, cut into 2 x ½-inch strips

2 teaspoons olive oil

4 scallions, cut into 1-inch lengths

4 cloves garlic, minced

1 green bell pepper, cut into 2 x ½-inch strips

1 red bell pepper, cut into 2 x ½-inch strips

½ pound sugar snap peas, strings removed

2 cups cherry tomatoes, halved

1. In a medium saucepan, bring 2¼ cups of water to a boil. Add the rice and ¼ teaspoon of the salt, reduce to a simmer, cover, and cook until the rice is tender, about 17 minutes.

2. Meanwhile, in a medium bowl, combine 1 teaspoon of the cornstarch, the broth, soy sauce, vinegar, sesame seeds, sesame oil, and sugar. Set aside.

3. Dredge the beef in the remaining 3 teaspoons cornstarch, shaking off the excess. In a large nonstick skillet, heat the oil until hot but not smoking over medium heat. Add the beef to the pan and cook, stirring frequently, until lightly browned, about 2 minutes. With a slotted spoon, transfer the beef to a plate.

4. Add the scallions and garlic to the pan and cook, stirring frequently, until crisp-tender, about 1 minute. Add the bell peppers, sugar snap peas, and tomatoes and cook, stirring frequently, until the tomatoes begin to collapse, about 3 minutes. Whisk the broth mixture to combine and pour into the skillet along with the remaining ¼ teaspoon salt. Bring to a boil and cook, stirring, until slightly thickened, about 1 minute. Return the beef to the pan and cook just until heated through, about 1 minute. Divide the rice among 4 plates, spoon the beef alongside, and serve.

Helpful hint: Fresh or frozen snow peas may be substituted for the sugar snap peas.

FAT: 7G/18%
CALORIES: 357
SATURATED FAT: 1.5G
CARBOHYDRATE: 52G
PROTEIN: 19G
CHOLESTEROL: 35MG
SODIUM: 837MG

44

In Korea, beef is by far the favorite meat. It is typically cut into thin slices or narrow strips and stir-fried, grilled, or braised. Sesame seeds (and sesame oil) are among the signature seasonings of Korean cuisine; in this recipe, they are blended with other characteristic Korean flavorings—soy sauce, garlic, and scallions. As in most of Asia, rice completes the meal.

A light coating of seasoned flour keeps these pork tenderloin cutlets flavorful and juicy as they're sautéed. The coating is seasoned with fennel seeds and red pepper flakes, a fine complement to the accompanying corn relish, which boasts a tangy honey-mustard dressing. Serve roasted or oven-fried potatoes to round out the main dish.

FENNEL-CRUSTED PORK WITH CORN-PEPPER RELISH

SERVES: 4
WORKING TIME: 20 MINUTES
TOTAL TIME: 20 MINUTES

2 tablespoons red wine vinegar

4 teaspoons olive oil

2 teaspoons Dijon mustard

1 teaspoon honey

¾ teaspoon salt

2 cups frozen corn kernels, thawed

2 scallions, thinly sliced

1 red bell pepper, cut into ¼-inch dice

1 green bell pepper, cut into ¼-inch dice

3 tablespoons flour

¾ teaspoon fennel seeds, crushed

¼ teaspoon red pepper flakes

1 egg white beaten with 2 teaspoons water

¾ pound well-trimmed pork tenderloin, cut into 4 slices and pounded (see page 8) ½ inch thick

1. In a medium bowl, combine the vinegar, 1 teaspoon of the oil, the mustard, honey, and ¼ teaspoon of the salt. Add the corn, scallions, and bell peppers, stirring to combine. Set aside.

2. In a pie plate or shallow bowl, combine the remaining ½ teaspoon salt, the flour, fennel, and red pepper flakes. Place the egg white mixture in a shallow bowl. Dip the pork in the egg white (see tip; top photo), then dredge in the flour mixture, pressing the mixture into the meat (bottom photo).

3. In a large nonstick skillet, heat the remaining 3 teaspoons oil until hot but not smoking over medium heat. Add the pork and cook until browned, crisped, and cooked through, about 2 minutes per side. Transfer the pork to 4 plates, spoon the corn relish over, and serve.

Helpful hint: The corn-pepper relish can be prepared up to 24 hours in advance. Refrigerate it in a covered bowl.

FAT: 8G/27%
CALORIES: 263
SATURATED FAT: 1.7G
CARBOHYDRATE: 27G
PROTEIN: 22G
CHOLESTEROL: 55MG
SODIUM: 533MG

TIP

Dip each pork cutlet in the egg white mixture, turning it to coat completely. Then dredge the cutlet in the seasoned flour, patting and pressing the coating so that it adheres to the meat.

Beef and Vegetable Stir-Fry

Serves: 4
Working time: 25 minutes
Total time: 25 minutes

*R*ather than serving this stir-fry over rice, we've tossed the beef and vegetables—asparagus, carrots, and bell pepper—with freshly cooked fettuccine for a delightfully colorful dish. Chicken broth, lightly thickened with cornstarch and seasoned with sesame oil and ground ginger, forms a glossy, delicate sauce. Quick and simple to prepare, this stir-fry is great for casual entertaining.

8 ounces fettuccine

2 tablespoons flour

¾ teaspoon salt

¼ teaspoon freshly ground black pepper

½ pound well-trimmed top round of beef, cut into 2 x ½-inch strips

1 tablespoon olive oil

1 onion, halved and thinly sliced

2 carrots, halved lengthwise and thinly sliced

1 red bell pepper, cut into 2 x ½-inch strips

¾ pound asparagus, tough ends trimmed, cut into 2-inch lengths

1¼ cups reduced-sodium chicken broth, defatted

1¼ teaspoons cornstarch

1 teaspoon dark Oriental sesame oil

¾ teaspoon ground ginger

1. In a large pot of boiling water, cook the pasta until just tender. Drain well. Meanwhile, on a sheet of waxed paper, combine the flour, ¼ teaspoon of the salt, and the black pepper. Dredge the beef in the flour mixture, shaking off the excess. In a large non-stick skillet, heat the olive oil until hot but not smoking over medium-high heat. Add the beef and cook, stirring frequently, until lightly browned, about 1 minute. With a slotted spoon, transfer the beef to a plate.

2. Add the onion to the skillet, reduce the heat to medium, and cook, stirring frequently, until softened, about 5 minutes. Add the carrots and bell pepper and cook, stirring frequently, until the carrots are crisp-tender, about 3 minutes. Add the asparagus and ¼ cup of the broth and cook, stirring, until the asparagus are crisp-tender, about 3 minutes.

3. In a small bowl, combine the cornstarch, the remaining 1 cup broth, the sesame oil, ginger, and the remaining ½ teaspoon salt, whisking to blend. Stir into the skillet, bring to a boil, and return the beef to the pan. Cook, stirring, until slightly thickened, about 1 minute. Toss with the hot pasta and serve.

Helpful hint: The vegetables can be cut up in advance, wrapped separately, and refrigerated.

Fat: 9g/20%
Calories: 403
Saturated Fat: 1.8g
Carbohydrate: 55g
Protein: 25g
Cholesterol: 86mg
Sodium: 645mg

SPICY STIR-FRIED PORK WITH WATERCRESS

SERVES: 4
WORKING TIME: 30 MINUTES
TOTAL TIME: 30 MINUTES

*T*he richness of pork is set off by peppery watercress and the tang of tomatoes here. Make the dish as hot (or mild) as you like.

1 cup long-grain rice

¾ teaspoon salt

½ pound well-trimmed pork loin, cut into 2 x ¼-inch strips

4 teaspoons cornstarch

2 teaspoons olive oil

1 red onion, halved and thinly sliced

3 cloves garlic, minced

6 cups watercress, tough stems removed

½ teaspoon sugar

½ teaspoon hot pepper sauce

½ cup reduced-sodium chicken broth, defatted

2 cups cherry tomatoes, halved

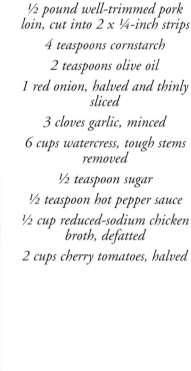

1. In a medium saucepan, bring 2¼ cups of water to a boil. Add the rice and ¼ teaspoon of the salt, reduce to a simmer, cover, and cook until the rice is tender, about 17 minutes. Meanwhile, dredge the pork in 3 teaspoons of the cornstarch, shaking off the excess. In a large skillet, heat the oil until hot but not smoking over medium heat. Add the pork and cook, stirring frequently, until lightly browned and just cooked through, about 2 minutes. With a slotted spoon, transfer the pork to a plate.

2. Add the onion and garlic to the pan and cook, stirring frequently, until the onion is crisp-tender, about 4 minutes. Add the watercress, sprinkle with the sugar, hot pepper sauce, and the remaining ½ teaspoon salt and cook, stirring frequently, until the watercress is wilted, about 3 minutes. Add the broth, bring to a boil, and stir in the tomatoes. Cook until the tomatoes begin to collapse, about 2 minutes.

3. In a small bowl, combine the remaining 1 teaspoon cornstarch and 1 tablespoon of water. Add to the skillet along with the pork and cook, stirring, until the sauce is slightly thickened and the pork is heated through, about 1 minute. Divide the rice among 4 plates, spoon the pork mixture alongside, and serve.

Helpful hint: If you're not sure that ½ teaspoon of hot pepper sauce will suit your taste buds, start with a few drops and add more as desired.

FAT: 6G/17%
CALORIES: 321
SATURATED FAT: 1.5G
CARBOHYDRATE: 48G
PROTEIN: 18G
CHOLESTEROL: 34MG
SODIUM: 561MG

STIR-FRIED BEEF WITH GREEN PEPPER SAUCE

SERVES: 4
WORKING TIME: 15 MINUTES
TOTAL TIME: 30 MINUTES

8 ounces linguine

2 green bell peppers, quartered lengthwise and seeded

3 cloves garlic, peeled

½ cup packed fresh parsley leaves

½ cup frozen peas, thawed

1 slice (1 ounce) firm-textured white bread

2 tablespoons capers, rinsed and drained

⅔ cup reduced-sodium chicken broth, defatted

2 tablespoons flour

½ teaspoon salt

10 ounces well-trimmed beef sirloin, cut into 2 x ¼-inch strips

1 tablespoon olive oil

1 red bell pepper, cut into strips

1. In a large pot of boiling water, cook the linguine until just tender. Drain well.

2. Meanwhile, preheat the broiler. Place the green bell peppers, cut-sides down, on the broiler rack. Broil the peppers 4 inches from the heat for about 10 minutes, or until the skin is blackened. When cool enough to handle, peel the peppers. Transfer the green bell peppers to a food processor. Add the garlic, parsley, peas, bread, and capers and process until well combined. Add the broth and process until smooth, about 1 minute.

3. On a sheet of waxed paper, combine the flour and salt. Dredge the beef in the flour mixture, shaking off the excess. In a large nonstick skillet, heat the oil until hot but not smoking over medium-high heat. Add the beef and cook, stirring frequently, until no longer pink, about 1 minute. Stir in the red bell pepper strips and the green pepper sauce and cook just until heated through, about 3 minutes. Toss with the pasta, divide among 4 bowls, and serve.

Helpful hint: To make it easier to peel the broiled peppers, transfer them directly from the oven to a bowl; cover and let stand for a few minutes to steam. This helps loosen the skins.

FAT: 8G/18%
CALORIES: 408
SATURATED FAT: 1.7G
CARBOHYDRATE: 57G
PROTEIN: 26G
CHOLESTEROL: 43MG
SODIUM: 668MG

This thick puréed sauce, made with roasted bell peppers, green peas, garlic, and capers, is practically fat-free.

HOT AND SOUR STIR-FRIED PORK

SERVES: 4
WORKING TIME: 25 MINUTES
TOTAL TIME: 35 MINUTES

The much-loved flavors of hot and sour soup work equally well to season the stir-fried strips of pork tenderloin, mushrooms, tomatoes, and scallions here. Dried mushrooms, an important ingredient in hot and sour soup, contribute their intense flavor to the sauce, abetted by rice vinegar, hot pepper sauce, and the warming pungency of ginger.

1 cup long-grain rice

¾ teaspoon salt

½ cup dried mushrooms, such as porcini, shiitake, or Polish

1 cup boiling water

10 ounces well-trimmed pork tenderloin, cut into 2 x ¼-inch strips

4 teaspoons cornstarch

1 tablespoon olive oil

5 scallions, cut into 1-inch lengths

¾ pound fresh shiitake or button mushrooms, thinly sliced

½ pound plum tomatoes, cut into 6 wedges each

¾ cup reduced-sodium chicken broth, defatted

2 tablespoons rice or cider vinegar

1 teaspoon hot pepper sauce

½ teaspoon ground ginger

1. In a medium saucepan, bring 2¼ cups of water to a boil. Add the rice and ¼ teaspoon of the salt, reduce to a simmer, cover, and cook until the rice is tender, about 17 minutes. Meanwhile, in a small bowl, combine the dried mushrooms and boiling water and let stand until softened, about 10 minutes. Reserving the soaking liquid, rinse and coarsely chop the mushrooms. Strain the liquid through a paper towel-lined sieve.

2. Dredge the pork in 3 teaspoons of the cornstarch, shaking off the excess. In a large nonstick skillet, heat the oil until hot but not smoking over medium heat. Add the pork and cook, stirring frequently, until lightly browned and just cooked through, about 2 minutes. With a slotted spoon, transfer the pork to a plate. Add the scallions to the skillet and cook, stirring frequently, until wilted, about 2 minutes. Add the reconstituted dried mushrooms, their soaking liquid, the fresh mushrooms, and tomatoes and cook until the fresh mushrooms are tender, about 4 minutes.

3. Add the broth, vinegar, hot pepper sauce, ginger, and the remaining ½ teaspoon salt. Bring to a boil and cook until the vegetables are tender, about 3 minutes. In a small bowl, stir together the remaining 1 teaspoon cornstarch and 1 tablespoon of water. Stir into the skillet along with the pork and cook, stirring, until slightly thickened, about 1 minute. Serve alongside the rice.

FAT: 6G/16%
CALORIES: 349
SATURATED FAT: 1.4G
CARBOHYDRATE: 51G
PROTEIN: 22G
CHOLESTEROL: 46MG
SODIUM: 597MG

Steak coated with cracked black peppercorns is a French bistro classic. The steak is usually topped with a knob of butter and flambéed with brandy; we've cut the fat (and toned down the performance) by making a brandy sauce in the pan after the steak is done. Creamy yet low in fat, the sauce gets its body from cornstarch and evaporated low-fat milk.

STEAK AU POIVRE WITH PEPPERS AND POTATOES

SERVES: 4
WORKING TIME: 25 MINUTES
TOTAL TIME: 30 MINUTES

1½ pounds small red potatoes, quartered

2 teaspoons coarsely cracked black pepper

½ teaspoon salt

¾ pound well-trimmed beef sirloin, cut into 4 steaks

4 teaspoons olive oil

3 bell peppers, mixed colors, cut into 2 x ¼-inch strips

¼ cup brandy

1 cup reduced-sodium beef broth, defatted

¼ cup evaporated low-fat (1%) milk

½ teaspoon dried thyme

1 teaspoon cornstarch mixed with 1 tablespoon water

1. In a medium pot of boiling water, cook the potatoes until firm-tender, about 12 minutes. Drain. Meanwhile, on a sheet of waxed paper, combine the cracked pepper and ¼ teaspoon of the salt. Coat both sides of the steaks with the pepper mixture (see tip). In a medium nonstick skillet, heat the oil until hot but not smoking over medium-high heat. Add the steaks and cook until well browned and crusty, about 2 minutes per side. Transfer the steaks to a plate.

2. Add the bell peppers to the skillet, reduce the heat to medium, and cook, stirring frequently, until crisp-tender, about 4 minutes. Remove the pan from the heat, add the brandy, and return to the heat. Cook until the brandy has almost evaporated, about 1 minute. Add the broth and cook until reduced by one-third, about 4 minutes.

3. Add the evaporated milk, thyme, and the remaining ¼ teaspoon salt to the pan and bring to a boil. Stir in the cornstarch mixture and cook, stirring, until slightly thickened, about 1 minute. Return the steaks to the pan and gently cook until heated through, about 2 minutes. Divide among 4 plates and serve with the potatoes.

Helpful hint: If evaporated low-fat milk isn't available, substitute evaporated skimmed milk.

FAT: 9G/22%
CALORIES: 362
SATURATED FAT: 1.9G
CARBOHYDRATE: 37G
PROTEIN: 24G
CHOLESTEROL: 54MG
SODIUM: 512MG

TIP

Place each steak in the cracked-pepper mixture and press the steak onto the pepper so that it adheres; then turn the steak and press the pepper into the other side.

Moroccan Spiced Pork Sauté

Serves: 4
Working time: 25 minutes
Total time: 30 minutes

1 cup long-grain rice

5 cloves garlic, minced

¾ teaspoon salt

¾ cup chopped fresh cilantro or basil

½ cup dried apricots, diced

2 tablespoons sliced almonds

2 tablespoons flour

½ pound well-trimmed center-cut pork loin, cut into 4 slices and pounded (see page 8) ½ inch thick

2 teaspoons olive oil

¾ teaspoon grated orange zest

¾ cup orange juice

1 teaspoon ground coriander

¾ teaspoon ground cumin

1¼ cups reduced-sodium chicken broth, defatted

1½ teaspoons cornstarch mixed with 1 tablespoon water

1. In a medium saucepan, bring 2¼ cups of water to a boil. Add the rice, 2 cloves of the garlic, and ¼ teaspoon of the salt, reduce to a simmer, cover, and cook until the rice is tender, about 17 minutes. Stir in the cilantro, apricots, and almonds; set the pilaf aside.

2. Meanwhile, on a sheet of waxed pepper, combine the flour and ¼ teaspoon of the salt. Dredge the pork in the flour mixture, shaking off the excess. In a large nonstick skillet, heat the oil until hot but not smoking over medium-high heat. Add the pork and cook until lightly browned, about 2 minutes per side. Transfer the pork to a plate.

3. Reduce the heat to medium, add the remaining 3 cloves of garlic, and cook, stirring frequently, until softened, about 2 minutes. Add the orange zest, orange juice, coriander, cumin, and the remaining ¼ teaspoon salt and cook, scraping up any browned bits that cling to the pan, until slightly reduced, about 2 minutes.

4. Add the broth to the pan and bring to a boil. Stir in the cornstarch mixture and cook, stirring, until sightly thickened, about 1 minute. Return the pork to the pan and cook just until cooked through, about 1 minute. Divide the pilaf among 4 plates. Place the pork alongside, spoon the sauce over, and serve.

Helpful hint: You'll need 2 to 3 oranges for ¾ cup juice.

Fat: 7g/17%
Calories: 376
Saturated Fat: 1.5g
Carbohydrate: 58g
Protein: 19g
Cholesterol: 36mg
Sodium: 632mg

We've based this pork sauté on the Moroccan way of cooking lamb, with aromatic spices, such as cumin and coriander, and garlic. The colorful pilaf also draws from traditional Moroccan ingredients; fresh cilantro, sliced almonds, dried apricots, oranges, and yet more heady garlic. Serve a mixed green salad alongside to complete the meal.

This Chinese-American classic was reputedly created by Chinese cooks in California in the 19th century. The dish became an American family favorite in the 1940s and '50s—but without real Chinese ingredients, which were hard to get back then. Our version, made with Napa cabbage, fresh ginger, and soy sauce, restores some of its Asian authenticity.

PORK CHOP SUEY

SERVES: 4
WORKING TIME: 25 MINUTES
TOTAL TIME: 30 MINUTES

1 cup long-grain rice

¾ teaspoon salt

4 teaspoons cornstarch

½ pound well-trimmed pork tenderloin, cut into 2 x ¼-inch strips

1 tablespoon vegetable oil

3 ribs celery, thinly sliced on the diagonal

½ pound mushrooms, thinly sliced

1 cup reduced-sodium chicken broth, defatted

3 scallions, thinly sliced

2 tablespoons finely chopped fresh ginger

2 cups shredded Napa cabbage (see tip) or green cabbage

8-ounce can sliced bamboo shoots, rinsed and drained

2 tablespoons reduced-sodium soy sauce

1 teaspoon sugar

1. In a medium saucepan, bring 2¼ cups of water to a boil. Add the rice and ¼ teaspoon of the salt, reduce to a simmer, cover, and cook until the rice is tender, about 17 minutes.

2. Meanwhile, on a sheet of waxed paper, combine 3 teaspoons of the cornstarch and ¼ teaspoon of the salt. Dredge the pork in the cornstarch mixture, shaking off the excess. In a large nonstick skillet, heat the oil until hot but not smoking over medium-high heat. Add the pork and cook, stirring frequently, until lightly browned, about 2 minutes. With a slotted spoon, transfer the pork to a plate.

3. Add the celery, mushrooms, and ¼ cup of the broth to the pan and cook until the celery is crisp-tender, about 4 minutes. Add the scallions and ginger and cook, stirring frequently, until the scallions are tender, about 2 minutes. Add the cabbage and bamboo shoots and cook until the cabbage is just wilted, about 2 minutes.

4. In a small bowl, combine the remaining 1 teaspoon cornstarch with the remaining ¾ cup broth, the soy sauce, sugar, and the remaining ¼ teaspoon salt. Pour into the skillet, bring to a boil, and cook, stirring, until slightly thickened, about 1 minute. Return the pork to the pan and cook just until heated through, about 1 minute. Divide the rice among 4 plates, spoon the pork chop suey over, and serve.

FAT: 6G/17%
CALORIES: 327
SATURATED FAT: 1.2G
CARBOHYDRATE: 49G
PROTEIN: 19G
CHOLESTEROL: 37MG
SODIUM: 919MG

TIP

To shred Napa cabbage, first remove each leaf individually. Stack three to four leaves at a time and, with a large chef's knife, trim off and discard the tough ends. Then cut the stacked leaves crosswise into thin shreds about ¼ inch wide.

BEEF AND MACARONI SKILLET DINNER

SERVES: 4
WORKING TIME: 35 MINUTES
TOTAL TIME: 35 MINUTES

Those prepackaged meals-in-a-skillet mixes sure are tempting when you're short on time. But they don't compare with the fresh onions, peppers, scallions, and sharp Cheddar found here. And do you really want additives and preservatives on your dinner plate? It's well worth a few extra minutes to stir up this deliciously satisfying meal from scratch.

8 ounces ditalini pasta

2 teaspoons olive oil

1 onion, finely chopped

3 cloves garlic, minced

1 red bell pepper, cut into ½-inch squares

1 green bell pepper, cut into ½-inch squares

½ pound well-trimmed top round of beef, cut into chunks

2 teaspoons chili powder

1 teaspoon salt

14½-ounce can no-salt-added stewed tomatoes, chopped with their juices

3 tablespoons no-salt-added tomato paste

½ cup shredded Cheddar cheese (2 ounces)

1 scallion, thinly sliced

1. In a large pot of boiling water, cook the pasta until just tender. Drain well.

2. Meanwhile, in a large nonstick skillet, heat the oil until hot but not smoking over medium heat. Add the onion and garlic and cook, stirring frequently, until the onion is softened, about 5 minutes. Add the bell peppers and cook, stirring frequently, until crisp-tender, about 4 minutes.

3. In a food processor, process the beef until finely ground, about 30 seconds. Add to the skillet along with the chili powder and salt and cook, stirring frequently, until the beef is no longer pink, about 4 minutes. Stir in the tomatoes and tomato paste and bring to a boil. Reduce to a simmer and cook, stirring occasionally, until the flavors have blended, about 5 minutes.

4. Stir the drained ditalini into the skillet and cook until heated through, about 3 minutes. Sprinkle the Cheddar and scallion over and heat without stirring until the cheese has just melted, about 1 minute.

Helpful hint: Elbow macaroni or small pasta shells can be substituted for the ditalini, if you like.

FAT: 10G/21%
CALORIES: 431
SATURATED FAT: 4.1G
CARBOHYDRATE: 59G
PROTEIN: 26G
CHOLESTEROL: 47MG
SODIUM: 713MG

PORK SAUTÉ WITH CHIVE CREAM SAUCE

SERVES: 4
WORKING TIME: 25 MINUTES
TOTAL TIME: 25 MINUTES

This upscale one-pot main dish combines delicately browned pork tenderloin cutlets with an appealing mix of tender vegetables.

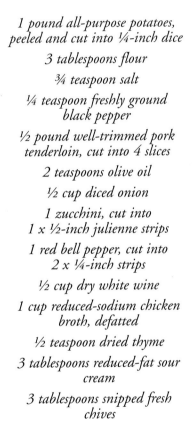

1 pound all-purpose potatoes, peeled and cut into ¼-inch dice

3 tablespoons flour

¾ teaspoon salt

¼ teaspoon freshly ground black pepper

½ pound well-trimmed pork tenderloin, cut into 4 slices

2 teaspoons olive oil

½ cup diced onion

1 zucchini, cut into 1 x ½-inch julienne strips

1 red bell pepper, cut into 2 x ¼-inch strips

½ cup dry white wine

1 cup reduced-sodium chicken broth, defatted

½ teaspoon dried thyme

3 tablespoons reduced-fat sour cream

3 tablespoons snipped fresh chives

1. In a large pot of boiling water, cook the potatoes until firm-tender, about 5 minutes. Drain.

2. Meanwhile, on a sheet of waxed paper, combine 2 tablespoons of the flour, ¼ teaspoon of the salt, and the black pepper. Dredge the pork in the flour mixture, shaking off the excess. In a large nonstick skillet, heat the oil until hot but not smoking over medium-high heat. Add the pork and cook until lightly browned, about 1 minute per side. Transfer the pork to a plate.

3. Add the onion to the skillet and cook, stirring frequently, until softened, about 2 minutes. Add the zucchini and bell pepper, stirring to coat. Add the wine and cook until reduced by one-third, about 2 minutes. Add the broth, thyme, potatoes, and the remaining ½ teaspoon salt. Bring to a boil, reduce to a simmer, and cook until the vegetables are tender, about 2 minutes.

4. In a small bowl, combine the sour cream and the remaining 1 tablespoon flour. Stir into the skillet along with the pork and cook, stirring occasionally, until the pork is just cooked through, the sauce is slightly thickened, and no floury taste remains, about 2 minutes. Place the pork on 4 plates. Stir the chives into the sauce, spoon over the pork, and serve.

Helpful hint: If you can't get fresh chives, substitute scallion greens.

FAT: 6G/23%
CALORIES: 239
SATURATED FAT: 1.7G
CARBOHYDRATE: 25G
PROTEIN: 17G
CHOLESTEROL: 41MG
SODIUM: 596MG

Sautéed Pork and Summer Squash

SERVES: 4
WORKING TIME: 25 MINUTES
TOTAL TIME: 30 MINUTES

1 cup long-grain rice

¾ teaspoon salt

2 tablespoons flour

½ teaspoon freshly ground black pepper

10 ounces well-trimmed pork tenderloin, cut into 8 slices and pounded (see page 8) ½ inch thick

1 tablespoon olive oil

4 cloves garlic, minced

1 yellow summer squash, quartered lengthwise and thinly sliced

1 zucchini, quartered lengthwise and thinly sliced

½ cup chopped fresh basil

¾ cup reduced-sodium chicken broth, defatted

1. In a medium saucepan, bring 2¼ cups of water to a boil. Add the rice and ¼ teaspoon of the salt, reduce to a simmer, cover, and cook until the rice is tender, about 17 minutes.

2. Meanwhile, on a sheet of waxed paper, combine the flour, the remaining ½ teaspoon salt, and the pepper. Dredge the pork in the flour mixture, shaking off the excess. In a large nonstick skillet, heat the oil until hot but not smoking over medium-high heat. Add the pork and cook until lightly browned, about 1 minute per side. Transfer the pork to a plate.

3. Reduce the heat to medium, add the garlic, and cook, stirring frequently, until softened, about 2 minutes. Add the yellow squash, zucchini, and basil and cook, stirring frequently, until the squash is crisp-tender, about 3 minutes. Add the broth and cook until the squash is very tender, about 3 minutes.

4. Return the pork to the pan and cook just until cooked through, about 1 minute. Divide the rice among 4 plates, spoon the pork and vegetables alongside, and serve.

Helpful hint: Thin-skinned summer squashes are not as sturdy as their winter counterparts. Whereas acorn or Hubbard squash will keep in a cool place for months, zucchini and yellow squash should be refrigerated in plastic bags for no longer than one week.

FAT: 6G/17%
CALORIES: 323
SATURATED FAT: 1.4G
CARBOHYDRATE: 45G
PROTEIN: 21G
CHOLESTEROL: 46MG
SODIUM: 558MG

Slices of summer squash, like translucent petals of green and gold, complement these delicate pork scallops.

Stir-Fried Beef with Green Beans and Pecans

SERVES: 4
WORKING TIME: 25 MINUTES
TOTAL TIME: 25 MINUTES

There's an innovative all-American twist to this Chinese-style dish. Instead of walnuts (which have been prized in China since ancient times), we've accented the dish with toasty-sweet pecans, which are native to this country. The chopped nuts echo the satisfying crunchiness of the water chestnuts and crisp-tender green beans.

8 ounces linguine

½ pound green beans, cut into 1-inch lengths

½ pound well-trimmed beef sirloin, cut into 2 x ½-inch strips

4 teaspoons cornstarch

1 tablespoon olive oil

3 tablespoons reduced-sodium soy sauce

2 cloves garlic, minced

2 tablespoons chopped fresh ginger

8-ounce can sliced water chestnuts, drained

¾ cup reduced-sodium chicken broth, defatted

¼ teaspoon salt

¼ teaspoon red pepper flakes

2 tablespoons coarsely chopped pecans (½ ounce)

1. In a large pot of boiling water, cook the pasta until just tender. Add the green beans during the last 3 minutes of cooking time. Drain well.

2. Meanwhile, dredge the beef in 3 teaspoons of the cornstarch. In a large nonstick skillet, heat the oil until hot but not smoking over medium-high heat. Add the beef and cook, stirring frequently, until lightly browned and cooked through, about 1 minute. With a slotted spoon, transfer the beef to a plate.

3. In a medium bowl, combine the soy sauce, garlic, ginger, and the remaining 1 teaspoon cornstarch; set aside. Add the linguine, green beans, and water chestnuts to the pan and cook, stirring frequently, until heated through, about 4 minutes. Return the beef to the pan along with the broth, salt, red pepper flakes, and the reserved soy sauce mixture and cook, stirring frequently, until slightly thickened, about 2 minutes. Stir in the pecans, divide among 4 plates, and serve.

Helpful hint: For extra flavor, toast the pecans: Spread them in a small baking pan and bake in a 350° oven for 8 to 10 minutes, shaking the pan occasionally to keep the nuts from scorching. As soon as the pecans are toasted, immediately tip them onto a plate to cool.

FAT: 9G/20%
CALORIES: 397
SATURATED FAT: 1.7G
CARBOHYDRATE: 56G
PROTEIN: 22G
CHOLESTEROL: 35MG
SODIUM: 735MG

BEEF STROGANOFF

SERVES: 4
WORKING TIME: 20 MINUTES
TOTAL TIME: 25 MINUTES

eef Stroganoff is a speedy dish by nature. The thin strips of beef need only moments in the skillet, and the sour cream sauce is quickly stirred up in the same pan. So we've concentrated on lowering the fat content, using a little olive oil in place of lots of butter and incorporating a modest amount of reduced-fat sour cream.

8 ounces wide egg noodles

2 tablespoons flour

1 tablespoon paprika

¾ teaspoon salt

½ teaspoon freshly ground black pepper

10 ounces well-trimmed top round of beef, cut into 2 x ½-inch strips

2 teaspoons olive oil

1 leek or 2 scallions, cut into 2 x ¼-inch julienne strips

2 carrots, peeled and cut into 2 x ¼-inch julienne strips

1⅓ cups reduced-sodium chicken broth, defatted

¼ cup gherkin pickles, rinsed, drained, and thinly sliced

¼ teaspoon dried rosemary, crumbled

3 tablespoons reduced-fat sour cream

1. In a large pot of boiling water, cook the noodles until just tender. Drain well.

2. Meanwhile, on a sheet of waxed paper, combine the flour, paprika, ¼ teaspoon of the salt, and ¼ teaspoon of the pepper. Dredge the beef in the flour mixture, shaking off and reserving the excess. In a large nonstick skillet, heat the oil until hot but not smoking over medium heat. Add the beef and cook, stirring frequently, until browned, about 1 minute. With a slotted spoon, transfer the beef to a plate.

3. Add the leek, carrots, and ⅓ cup of the broth to the pan and cook until the carrots are crisp-tender, about 3 minutes. Add the pickles, stirring to coat. Add the remaining 1 cup broth, the rosemary, the remaining ½ teaspoon salt, and remaining ¼ teaspoon pepper. Bring to a boil, reduce to a simmer, and cook until the vegetables are tender, about 3 minutes.

4. In a small bowl, combine the sour cream and the reserved flour mixture. Stir into the pan along with the noodles and beef and cook until heated through and slightly thickened, about 2 minutes.

Helpful hint: To further reduce the cholesterol content of the Stroganoff, you can use yolkless egg noodles instead of the regular kind.

FAT: 9G/19%
CALORIES: 424
SATURATED FAT: 2.4G
CARBOHYDRATE: 58G
PROTEIN: 27G
CHOLESTEROL: 98MG
SODIUM: 781MG

*T*here's nothing humdrum about the chunky sauce—virtually a side dish in itself—that surrounds these pork cutlets. The combination of broccoli, oranges, and peanuts seems to suggest an Asian dish, but the seasonings are oregano and cayenne rather than soy sauce and ginger. Orzo pasta is the simple backdrop for the flavorful sauce.

PORK MEDALLIONS WITH ORANGES AND PEANUTS

SERVES: 4
WORKING TIME: 25 MINUTES
TOTAL TIME: 25 MINUTES

8 ounces orzo pasta

¾ teaspoon dried oregano

¾ teaspoon salt

¼ teaspoon cayenne pepper

10 ounces well-trimmed pork loin, cut into 4 slices

4¼ teaspoons cornstarch

2½ teaspoons olive oil

1 red bell pepper, cut into 2 x ¼-inch strips

1 onion, halved and thinly sliced

3 cloves garlic, slivered

1½ cups reduced-sodium chicken broth, defatted

2 cups small broccoli florets

½ teaspoon grated orange zest

2 navel oranges, peeled and sectioned, juices reserved (see tip)

4 teaspoons coarsely chopped peanuts

1. In a large pot of boiling water, cook the pasta until just tender. Drain well.

2. Meanwhile, in a small bowl, combine the oregano, salt, and cayenne. Sprinkle the pork with 1 teaspoon of the mixture, rubbing it into the meat (set the remaining spice mixture aside). Dredge the pork in 3 teaspoons of the cornstarch, shaking off the excess. In a large nonstick skillet, heat the oil until hot but not smoking over medium-high heat. Add the pork and cook until lightly browned and almost cooked through, about 1 minute per side. Transfer the pork to a plate.

3. Add the bell pepper, onion, and garlic to the skillet, reduce the heat to medium, and cook, stirring frequently, until the bell pepper is crisp-tender, about 3 minutes. Add the broth, broccoli, orange zest, and the reserved spice mixture. Bring to a boil, reduce to a simmer, and cook until the vegetables are tender, about 2 minutes.

4. In a small bowl, combine the remaining 1¼ teaspoons cornstarch and 1 tablespoon of water. Return the vegetable mixture in the skillet to a boil, stir in the cornstarch mixture, and cook, stirring, until slightly thickened, about 1 minute. Return the pork to the pan along with the oranges and their juices and the peanuts and cook just until heated through, about 1 minute. Divide the pasta among 4 plates, spoon the pork and sauce alongside, and serve.

FAT: 10G/20%
CALORIES: 449
SATURATED FAT: 2.1G
CARBOHYDRATE: 63G
PROTEIN: 28G
CHOLESTEROL: 42MG
SODIUM: 694MG

TIP

To prepare the oranges, remove the peel and, using a small knife, trim away all the bitter white pith. Working over a sieve set over a bowl to catch the juices, cut between the membranes to release the orange sections.

STIR-FRIED ITALIAN PORK AND RICE

SERVES: 4
WORKING TIME: 25 MINUTES
TOTAL TIME: 40 MINUTES

1⅓ cups long-grain rice

¾ teaspoon salt

2 teaspoons olive oil

¼ cup plus 2 tablespoons finely chopped prosciutto or Canadian bacon (2 ounces)

½ pound well-trimmed pork tenderloin, cut into 2 x ¼-inch strips

1 onion, halved and thinly sliced

3 cloves garlic, slivered

6 ounces mushrooms, thinly sliced

½ cup reduced-sodium chicken broth, defatted

½ cup chopped fresh basil

½ teaspoon freshly ground black pepper

1¼ cups frozen peas, thawed

¼ cup grated Parmesan cheese

1. In a medium saucepan, bring 3 cups of water to a boil. Add the rice and ¼ teaspoon of the salt, reduce to a simmer, cover, and cook until the rice is tender, about 17 minutes.

2. Meanwhile, in a large nonstick skillet, heat the oil until hot but not smoking over medium heat. Add the prosciutto and cook, stirring, until lightly crisped, about 2 minutes. Add the pork and cook, stirring frequently, until no longer pink and just cooked through, about 2 minutes. With a slotted spoon, transfer the pork to a plate.

3. Add the onion and garlic to the skillet and cook, stirring frequently, until the onion is lightly golden, about 4 minutes. Add the mushrooms, stirring to coat. Add the broth and cook, stirring frequently, until the mushrooms are tender and lightly browned, about 3 minutes. Add the rice, basil, the remaining ½ teaspoon salt, and the pepper and cook, stirring frequently, until the rice is lightly crisped and hot, about 5 minutes.

4. Return the pork to the pan along with the peas and cook until heated through, about 2 minutes. Stir in the Parmesan and serve.

Helpful Hint: The rice may be prepared up to a day ahead and refrigerated; if so, it may take a few minutes longer to reheat the rice in step 3.

FAT: 9G/19%
CALORIES: 438
SATURATED FAT: 2.6G
CARBOHYDRATE: 63G
PROTEIN: 27G
CHOLESTEROL: 52MG
SODIUM: 923MG

70

There's no reason to restrict your stir-frying to Chinese or Thai dishes. This quick, efficient cooking technique can be adapted to all sorts of cuisines. Here, prosciutto (Italian salt-cured ham) forms the flavor base for stir-fried pork and mushrooms; fresh basil and Parmesan render the dish unmistakably Italian. In a departure from tradition, the rice is stirred right into the skillet.

HAM AND POTATO HASH

SERVES: 4
WORKING TIME: 30 MINUTES
TOTAL TIME: 30 MINUTES

A

splendid homestyle supper, this sage-scented hash would also make a terrific brunch dish, with or without eggs.

1½ pounds all-purpose
potatoes, peeled and cut into
¼-inch dice

4 teaspoons olive oil

2 onions, finely chopped

2 green bell peppers, cut into
¼-inch dice

2 Granny Smith apples, cored
and cut into ¼-inch dice

5 ounces thinly sliced baked
ham, slivered

⅔ cup reduced-sodium chicken
broth, defatted

1 tablespoon Dijon mustard

½ teaspoon sage

¼ teaspoon salt

¼ teaspoon freshly ground
black pepper

1. In a large pot of boiling water, cook the potatoes until firm-tender, about 5 minutes. Drain.

2. Meanwhile, in a large nonstick skillet, heat the oil until hot but not smoking over medium heat. Add the onions and cook, stirring frequently, until lightly browned, about 5 minutes.

3. Add the bell peppers, apples, and potatoes to the pan and cook, stirring frequently, until the apples have softened, about 5 minutes. Add the ham and cook, stirring frequently, until crisped, about 4 minutes.

4. Stir the broth, mustard, sage, salt, and black pepper into the skillet and cook, stirring frequently, until the hash is richly flavored and slightly crusty, about 5 minutes. Divide among 4 plates and serve.

Helpful hint: You can cook the potatoes up to 12 hours in advance; drain them and refrigerate in a covered bowl. Bring the potatoes to room temperature before making the hash, and allow a little extra time for them to heat up in step 3.

FAT: 7G/23%
CALORIES: 280
SATURATED FAT: 1.3G
CARBOHYDRATE: 43G
PROTEIN: 12G
CHOLESTEROL: 19MG
SODIUM: 756MG

OVEN DISHES

3

The trick that turns this manicotti into a low-fat meal is the substitution of mashed potatoes for some of the cheese in the stuffing. Chopped pork, nonfat ricotta, bread crumbs, egg white, and Parmesan go into the filling as well; fresh basil adds a pesto-like flavor. Serve the manicotti with a light side dish, such as steamed zucchini and summer squash.

Baked Pork Manicotti

SERVES: 4
WORKING TIME: 30 MINUTES
TOTAL TIME: 1 HOUR

½ pound all-purpose potatoes, peeled and cut into 8 wedges each

12 manicotti shells (8 ounces)

14½-ounce can no-salt-added stewed tomatoes

8-ounce can no-salt-added tomato sauce

¾ cup packed basil leaves, chopped

¾ teaspoon salt

⅛ teaspoon freshly ground black pepper

½ pound well-trimmed pork tenderloin, cut into 1-inch cubes

3 scallions, finely chopped

½ cup fresh bread crumbs (from 1 slice of bread)

1 cup nonfat ricotta cheese

1 egg white

6 tablespoons grated Parmesan cheese

1. In a large pot of boiling water, cook the potatoes until firm-tender, about 10 minutes. With a slotted spoon, transfer the potatoes to a medium bowl and mash. Bring the water back to a boil, add the manicotti shells, and cook until almost tender. Drain, rinse under cold water, and drain again.

2. Meanwhile, preheat the oven to 425°. Spray a 13 x 9-inch baking dish with nonstick cooking spray. In a medium bowl, combine the stewed tomatoes, tomato sauce, ¼ cup of the basil, ¼ teaspoon of the salt, and the pepper. Spoon one-third of the sauce into the prepared baking dish.

3. Place the pork, scallions, and the remaining ½ cup basil in a food processor and process until the mixture is the size of small peas. Add the mashed potatoes, bread crumbs, ricotta, egg white, 4 tablespoons of the Parmesan, and the remaining ½ teaspoon salt and process until just combined. Pipe the mixture into the manicotti shells with a pastry bag or a sturdy plastic bag (see tip).

4. Arrange the manicotti in the baking dish and spoon the remaining sauce on top. Cover tightly with foil and bake for 30 minutes, or until heated through. Divide the manicotti among 4 plates, sprinkle the remaining 2 tablespoons Parmesan over, and serve.

FAT: 6G/11%
CALORIES: 477
SATURATED FAT: 2.3G
CARBOHYDRATE: 68G
PROTEIN: 35G
CHOLESTEROL: 43MG
SODIUM: 731MG

TIP

If you don't have a pastry bag, use a heavy-duty plastic bag to fill the manicotti. Spoon the mixture into the bag, then snip off one of the lower corners. Place the open tip in the pasta shell and squeeze the bag to pipe in the filling.

CHEESEBURGER PIZZAS

SERVES: 4
WORKING TIME: 15 MINUTES
TOTAL TIME: 30 MINUTES

Maybe you thought the only way to "slim down" pizza was to leave off the cheese. But these individual pizzas, topped with ground beef and two cheeses, have an impressively low total fat content. Cheddar and Parmesan have more flavor impact than mozzarella, so you can use less. Pair the pizzas with a big green salad; season the vinaigrette with a pinch of oregano.

3 tablespoons yellow cornmeal

1 pound store-bought pizza dough

6 ounces well-trimmed top round of beef, cut into chunks

15-ounce can no-salt-added whole tomatoes, coarsely chopped and drained

3 tablespoons ketchup

2 cloves garlic, minced

½ teaspoon dried thyme

¼ teaspoon red pepper flakes

2 scallions, sliced

¾ cup shredded Cheddar cheese (3 ounces)

3 tablespoons grated Parmesan cheese

1. Preheat the oven to 475°. Spray 2 baking sheets with nonstick cooking spray. Sprinkle each sheet evenly with the cornmeal. Divide the dough into 4 pieces and roll each piece into a 7-inch circle. Place 2 circles of dough on each of the prepared baking sheets. Bake for 6 minutes, or until cooked but not browned (the dough will puff up, but will collapse when removed from the oven). Leave the oven on.

2. Meanwhile, in a food processor, process the beef until finely ground. In a medium bowl, combine the tomatoes, ketchup, garlic, thyme, and red pepper flakes.

3. Spread the tomato mixture onto the cooked pizza bases. Crumble the beef evenly over the tops of the pizzas. Sprinkle with the scallions, Cheddar, and Parmesan. Bake for 8 minutes, or until the beef is cooked through and the cheeses are melted and bubbling. Remove and let stand for 5 minutes before dividing among 4 plates and serving.

Helpful hints: You can buy ready-to-use pizza dough from many pizzerias and Italian specialty stores; you may also find it in the dairy case in the supermarket. Or, you can use the refrigerated dough that comes in a roll.

FAT: 14G/25%
CALORIES: 507
SATURATED FAT: 6.5G
CARBOHYDRATE: 67G
PROTEIN: 28G
CHOLESTEROL: 50MG
SODIUM: 997MG

*S*tuffed
cabbage minus the fuss
and bother—that's the
definition of this
simplified classic.
Rather than filling
and folding individual
cabbage rolls, you line
a pie plate with
cabbage leaves, spoon
in the filling, and
cover with more leaves
to make a "pie." The
size of the cabbage
leaves will determine
how many you'll need:
We used ten large
leaves.

Cabbage Pie

SERVES: 4
WORKING TIME: 30 MINUTES
TOTAL TIME: 1 HOUR 5 MINUTES

8 to 12 large cabbage leaves

¾ cup reduced-sodium beef broth, defatted

1 sweet onion, such as Vidalia, finely chopped

2 carrots, shredded

2 cloves garlic, minced

½ teaspoon caraway seeds

½ teaspoon dried thyme

1¼ cups quick-cooking brown rice

6 ounces well-trimmed top round of beef, cut into 1-inch cubes

6 ounces well-trimmed pork tenderloin, cut into 1-inch cubes

1 egg white, lightly beaten

1 tablespoon Dijon mustard

1 teaspoon ground ginger

¼ teaspoon salt

1. In a large pot of boiling water, cook the cabbage leaves until tender and pliable, 2 to 4 minutes. Drain well.

2. Meanwhile, in a medium saucepan, combine the broth, ¼ cup of water, the onion, carrots, garlic, caraway, and thyme. Bring to a simmer and cook for 8 minutes. Stir in the rice, cover, and cook for 5 minutes. Transfer to a large bowl and set aside to cool slightly.

3. Preheat the oven to 400°. Spray a 9-inch pie plate with nonstick cooking spray. In a food processor, combine the beef and pork and process until finely chopped. Add the beef mixture to the cooled rice mixture along with the egg white, mustard, ginger, and salt, stirring until well combined.

4. Cover the bottom of the pie plate with 4 to 6 cabbage leaves, overlapping them and leaving an overhang of 2 inches all around (see tip; top photo). Spoon the rice mixture over the cabbage leaves, mounding it in the center. Cover the top of the rice mixture with the remaining cabbage leaves (middle photo), then fold up the overhanging leaves to cover the top (bottom photo). Cover the pie tightly with foil that has been sprayed with nonstick cooking spray and bake for 45 minutes, or until heated through. Cut the cabbage pie into wedges, divide among 4 plates, and serve.

FAT: 5G/14%
CALORIES: 314
SATURATED FAT: 1G
CARBOHYDRATE: 45G
PROTEIN: 26G
CHOLESTEROL: 52MG
SODIUM: 456MG

TIP

BEEF MOUSSAKA

SERVES: 4
WORKING TIME: 30 MINUTES
TOTAL TIME: 1 HOUR

6 ounces well-trimmed top round of beef, cut into chunks
6 ounces orzo pasta
1 teaspoon olive oil
2 zucchini, coarsely chopped
1 onion, coarsely chopped
2 cloves garlic, minced
¾ teaspoon dried oregano
½ teaspoon dried tarragon
½ teaspoon hot pepper sauce
Two 8-ounce cans no-salt-added tomato sauce
3 tablespoons no-salt-added tomato paste
1 cup frozen peas
½ teaspoon salt
1 cup part-skim ricotta cheese
1 egg white
½ cup low-fat (1%) milk
¼ cup grated Parmesan cheese

1. Preheat the oven to 400°. Spray an 11 x 7-inch baking dish with nonstick cooking spray. In a food processor, process the beef until coarsely ground.

2. In a large pot of boiling water, cook the orzo until just tender. Drain, rinse under cold water, and drain again.

3. Meanwhile, in a large nonstick skillet, heat the oil until hot but not smoking over medium heat. Add the zucchini, onion, and garlic and cook, stirring frequently, until the onion is tender, about 10 minutes. Stir in the oregano, tarragon, and hot pepper sauce and cook until fragrant, about 1 minute. Stir in the tomato sauce, tomato paste, beef, peas, and salt. Simmer until slightly thickened, about 2 minutes.

4. In a blender or food processor, combine the ricotta, egg white, milk, and 2 tablespoons of the Parmesan and blend until smooth. Spoon the orzo into the prepared baking dish. Top with the meat mixture. Spoon the ricotta mixture over and sprinkle with the remaining 2 tablespoons Parmesan. Bake for 35 minutes, or until the topping is bubbly and golden brown. Divide among 4 plates and serve.

Helpful hint: This dish is often made with lamb, and you could substitute chunks of leg of lamb or the leaner hind shank for the beef.

FAT: 11G/22%
CALORIES: 458
SATURATED FAT: 5G
CARBOHYDRATE: 59G
PROTEIN: 32G
CHOLESTEROL: 49MG
SODIUM: 591MG

We've given this beloved Greek casserole a thorough but thoughtful make-over. Instead of a layer of fried potatoes or eggplant, we've built the dish on a base of orzo. We've substituted lean ground beef for fattier lamb, and totally revamped the traditional egg-rich topping: Our version is made with part-skim ricotta, low-fat milk, and egg white.

BAKED CINCINNATI CHILI

SERVES: 4
WORKING TIME: 25 MINUTES
TOTAL TIME: 50 MINUTES

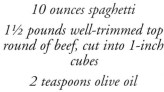

Ohio's famous chili is unique: Seasoned with both sweet and hot spices, it's served over spaghetti and topped with Cheddar.

10 ounces spaghetti

1½ pounds well-trimmed top round of beef, cut into 1-inch cubes

2 teaspoons olive oil

2 cloves garlic, minced

2 onions, coarsely chopped

1 green bell pepper, coarsely chopped

2 tablespoons chili powder

1 tablespoon ground cumin

2 teaspoons unsweetened cocoa powder

14½-ounce can no-salt-added stewed tomatoes

8-ounce can no-salt-added tomato sauce

1 tablespoon red wine vinegar

1 tablespoon Worcestershire sauce

¾ teaspoon salt

½ teaspoon hot pepper sauce

¼ cup grated Cheddar cheese

1. In a large pot of boiling water, cook the spaghetti until just tender. Drain well.

2. Preheat the oven to 400°. Spray a shallow 3-quart casserole with nonstick cooking spray. Place the beef in a food processor and process until the size of small peas.

3. Meanwhile, in a large nonstick skillet, heat the oil until hot but not smoking over medium heat. Add the garlic, onions, and bell pepper and cook, stirring, until the onion is tender, about 8 minutes. Stir in the chili powder, cumin, and cocoa powder and cook until fragrant, about 1 minute. Stir in the stewed tomatoes, tomato sauce, vinegar, Worcestershire sauce, salt, and hot pepper sauce; bring to a simmer, stir in the chopped beef, and cook until heated through, about 2 minutes.

4. In a large bowl, combine the beef mixture and spaghetti and add to the prepared casserole. Cover with foil and bake for 20 minutes, or until the chili is piping hot. Remove the foil, sprinkle the cheese over, and bake 5 minutes, or until the cheese is melted. Divide among 4 plates and serve.

Helpful hint: You can prepare the beef mixture up to one day in advance and refrigerate it in a covered container. Reheat the beef mixture while you cook the spaghetti.

FAT: 13G/18%
CALORIES: 639
SATURATED FAT: 4G
CARBOHYDRATE: 77G
PROTEIN: 54G
CHOLESTEROL: 105MG
SODIUM: 681MG

ONION-SMOTHERED BEEF

SERVES: 4
WORKING TIME: 20 MINUTES
TOTAL TIME: 1 HOUR 10 MINUTES

3 cloves garlic, minced

3 scallions, finely chopped

2 tablespoons mild paprika

1½ teaspoons dried thyme

1 teaspoon dried basil

1 teaspoon honey

¾ teaspoon salt

*¼ teaspoon freshly ground
black pepper*

*1¼ pounds well-trimmed top
round of beef*

4 onions, thinly sliced

*½ cup reduced-sodium beef
broth, defatted*

¼ cup dry sherry

*1½ pounds small red potatoes,
quartered*

1. Preheat the oven to 400°. Spray a 13 x 9-inch baking dish or roasting pan with nonstick cooking spray. In a small bowl, combine the garlic, scallions, paprika, thyme, basil, honey, salt, and pepper. Rub about half of this mixture into the beef and set the meat aside. Place the onion slices in the prepared pan, sprinkle with the remaining spice mixture, and pour the broth and sherry over.

2. Spray another 13 x 9-inch baking dish or roasting pan with nonstick cooking spray. Place the potatoes in one layer in the dish and cover with foil. Place the potatoes and onions in the oven and roast for 30 minutes. Place the beef on top of the onions and roast for 20 minutes, or until the potatoes are firm-tender, the onions are very tender, and the beef is medium-rare.

3. Transfer the beef to a cutting board and let stand for at least 10 minutes before slicing. Divide the sliced beef among 4 plates, top with the onions, place the potatoes alongside, and serve.

Helpful hint: For a more casual meal, instead of roasting potatoes, serve the beef and onions on big, crusty rolls.

FAT: 6G/13%
CALORIES: 412
SATURATED FAT: 1.7G
CARBOHYDRATE: 52G
PROTEIN: 39G
CHOLESTEROL: 81MG
SODIUM: 588MG

Roasted beef with a spicy-sweet crust, sherry-braised onions, and roasted potatoes make this meal a standout.

83

PORK, HAM, AND RICE PILAF

SERVES: 4
WORKING TIME: 20 MINUTES
TOTAL TIME: 40 MINUTES

*B*rowning the rice in oil before it's simmered or steamed in broth gives it a deliciously nutlike, robust flavor and coats the grains so that they remain separate when cooked. In this hearty pilaf, ham and pork tenderloin are added to the rice; the addition of kidney beans and peas makes this pilaf particularly rich in protein, and it's quite a substantial main dish in itself.

2 teaspoons olive oil
1 red onion, chopped
1 rib celery, chopped
2 cloves garlic, minced
2 ounces coarsely chopped reduced-sodium ham
6 ounces well-trimmed pork tenderloin, cut into ½-inch cubes
1 cup long-grain rice
13¾-ounce can reduced-sodium chicken broth, defatted
½ cup dry white wine
1 teaspoon dried marjoram
¼ teaspoon dried tarragon
½ teaspoon hot pepper sauce
¼ teaspoon salt
1 cup frozen peas, thawed
15-ounce can kidney beans, rinsed and drained
2 teaspoons Worcestershire sauce

1. Preheat the oven to 350°. In a Dutch oven or flameproof casserole, heat the oil until hot but not smoking over medium heat. Add the onion, celery, garlic, and ham and cook, stirring occasionally, until the onion is softened, about 7 minutes. Add the pork and cook, stirring frequently, until no longer pink, about 4 minutes.

2. Add the rice to the casserole, stirring to coat. Add the broth, wine, ½ cup of water, the marjoram, tarragon, hot pepper sauce, and salt. Bring to a boil over medium heat. Cover, place the casserole in the oven, and bake for 20 minutes, or until the rice is tender.

3. Add the peas, kidney beans, and Worcestershire sauce to the casserole, stirring to evenly distribute. Re-cover and let stand until the peas and beans are heated through, about 1 minute. Divide among 4 plates and serve.

Helpful hint: If you prefer not to use wine, simply substitute another ½ cup of broth.

FAT: 5G/11%
CALORIES: 409
SATURATED FAT: 1.1G
CARBOHYDRATE: 60G
PROTEIN: 24G
CHOLESTEROL: 34MG
SODIUM: 749MG

Butterflied meat is often stuffed, rolled, and tied for roasting or baking. Here, flank steak is filled with an herbed bread-and-corn stuffing and basted with a chili sauce. Prepare a simple vegetable side dish, such as sautéed broccoli and red pepper strips, to complete the meal.

Rolled Flank Steak

Serves: 4
Working time: 20 minutes
Total time: 1 hour 30 minutes

4 scallions, chopped

2 cups frozen corn kernels

2 cups fresh bread crumbs (from 4 slices of bread)

⅓ cup chopped fresh parsley

1 egg white

¼ cup reduced-sodium chicken broth, defatted

¾ teaspoon dried thyme

1¼ teaspoons dried sage

½ teaspoon salt

¾-pound well-trimmed flank steak, butterflied (see tip; top photo) and pounded to a ¼-inch thickness

⅓ cup chili sauce

2 tablespoons honey

2 tablespoons Worcestershire sauce

1. Preheat the oven to 350°. Spray an 11 x 7-inch baking dish with nonstick cooking spray.

2. In a large bowl, combine the scallions, corn, bread crumbs, and parsley. In a small bowl, combine the egg white, broth, thyme, ¾ teaspoon of the sage, and the salt. Stir the broth mixture into the stuffing.

3. Spread the stuffing evenly over the flank steak, leaving a ½-inch border all around. Roll the flank steak up (see tip; middle photo) and tie in several places with kitchen string (bottom photo). In a small bowl, combine the chili sauce, honey, Worcestershire sauce, and the remaining ½ teaspoon sage. Place the rolled steak in the prepared baking dish and brush with half of the chili sauce mixture.

4. Bake the steak for 1 hour, or until the meat is medium-rare. Baste with the remaining chili sauce halfway during the cooking. Let stand for 15 minutes before slicing. Divide the slices among 4 plates and serve.

Helpful hint: To butterfly flank steak, use a very sharp knife to slice the steak horizontally, stopping just short of cutting all the way through. Open the steak like a book, place it on a cutting board, and pound with the flat side of a meat pounder or a small heavy skillet until it is ¼ inch thick.

Fat: 8g/21%
Calories: 343
Saturated Fat: 3g
Carbohydrate: 46g
Protein: 24g
Cholesterol: 44mg
Sodium: 890mg

TIP

Roasted Honey-Mustard Pork with Stuffing

SERVES: 4
WORKING TIME: 10 MINUTES
TOTAL TIME: 45 MINUTES

*S*ome people would call this "dressing" rather than "stuffing" because it's cooked under pork cutlets, not inside chops. Whatever you choose to call it, the sweetly savory mixture is a unique one—a combination of bread, chopped prunes, chunks of apple, and bits of pimiento, moistened with honey, mustard, and broth. The pork, spread with honey-mustard, cooks up tender and juicy.

2 tablespoons plus 1 teaspoon Dijon mustard

2 teaspoons honey

⅓ cup reduced-sodium chicken broth, defatted

4 slices (1 ounce each) firm-textured white bread, crumbled

5 scallions, coarsely chopped

½ cup prunes, coarsely chopped

1 tart green apple, peeled, cored, and cut into ½-inch chunks

½ cup jarred pimientos, rinsed, drained, and chopped

¾ teaspoon dried rosemary, crumbled

¼ teaspoon freshly ground black pepper

¼ teaspoon salt

¾ pound well-trimmed pork tenderloin, cut into 4 slices and pounded (see page 8) ¾ inch thick

1. Preheat the oven to 400°. Spray a 9-inch square glass baking dish with nonstick cooking spray. In a small bowl, combine the mustard and honey. In a large bowl, combine the broth and 2 tablespoons of the honey-mustard. Add the bread, scallions, prunes, apple, pimientos, rosemary, pepper, and salt, stirring to combine. Spoon the stuffing mixture into the prepared casserole.

2. Place the pork on top of the stuffing and brush with the remaining 1 tablespoon honey-mustard. Bake for 30 to 35 minutes, or until the pork is cooked through but is still juicy and the stuffing is heated through. Divide the stuffing among 4 plates, top with the pork, and serve.

Helpful hint: For a change, you might like to substitute the same amount of dried cranberries or dried cherries for the chopped prunes.

FAT: 5G/16%
CALORIES: 279
SATURATED FAT: 1.2G
CARBOHYDRATE: 37G
PROTEIN: 22G
CHOLESTEROL: 56MG
SODIUM: 594MG

All over the world, turnovers and their kin are popular meals and snacks. Italian calzone, Mexican empanadas, Chinese pork buns, and Cornish pasties are all variations on the idea of a savory filling enclosed in dough. These turnovers feature a rich crust made with Neufchâtel cheese wrapped around a calzone-style filling of cheese, ham, and spinach.

HAM AND SPINACH TURNOVERS

SERVES: 4
WORKING TIME: 25 MINUTES
TOTAL TIME: 55 MINUTES

2 cups flour

1 tablespoon sugar

1 teaspoon baking powder

2 ounces reduced-fat cream
cheese (Neufchâtel)

4 teaspoons solid vegetable
shortening

¾ cup plain nonfat yogurt

1 cup low-fat (1%) cottage
cheese, preferably dry-curd

10-ounce package frozen
chopped spinach, thawed and
squeezed dry

3 scallions, finely chopped

¼ pound reduced-sodium ham,
minced

¼ cup chopped fresh basil

3 tablespoons plain dried bread
crumbs

1 tablespoon minced Calamata
or other brine-cured black olives

1 egg white, lightly beaten

½ teaspoon hot pepper sauce

1 tablespoon whole milk

1. In a large bowl, combine the flour, sugar, and baking powder. With a pastry blender or 2 knives, cut in the cream cheese and shortening until the mixture resembles coarse meal. Stir in the yogurt and 1 tablespoon of water just until the dough comes together. Divide into fourths, flatten into disks, wrap in plastic wrap, and chill for 20 minutes in the freezer.

2. Meanwhile, in a large bowl, combine the cottage cheese, spinach, scallions, ham, basil, bread crumbs, olives, egg white, and hot pepper sauce.

3. Preheat the oven to 400°. Spray a baking sheet with nonstick cooking spray. On a well floured surface, roll each piece of dough out to a 7-inch circle. Spoon one-fourth of the filling mixture onto half of each round to within ½ inch of the edges (see tip; top photo). Moisten the edges of the dough with water, fold in half (middle photo), and crimp the edges to seal (bottom photo). Brush the turnovers with the milk. Place the turnovers on the prepared baking sheet and bake for 20 minutes, or until lightly golden. Divide the turnovers among 4 plates and serve.

Helpful hint: The filling should be fairly dry, or the crust will be soggy. If you can't get dry-curd cottage cheese, place regular cottage cheese in a paper towel-lined sieve and let it drain for 5 to 10 minutes.

FAT: 11G/21%
CALORIES: 467
SATURATED FAT: 4.3G
CARBOHYDRATE: 65G
PROTEIN: 26G
CHOLESTEROL: 28MG
SODIUM: 845MG

TIP

"Sausage"-Stuffed Peppers

Serves: 4
Working time: 25 minutes
Total time: 1 hour 5 minutes

4 large bell peppers (about 8 ounces each)

½ pound well-trimmed pork tenderloin, cut into 1-inch cubes

½ teaspoon fennel seeds, lightly crushed

¼ teaspoon red pepper flakes

1 teaspoon olive oil

1½ cups reduced-sodium chicken broth, defatted

½ cup dry white wine

4 scallions, chopped

3 carrots, shredded

1 rib celery, finely chopped

1 teaspoon grated orange zest

¾ cup unseasoned white and wild rice mix

½ teaspoon salt

¼ cup grated Parmesan cheese

1. Slice the tops off the bell peppers and set aside, then remove and discard the seeds and ribs. In a large pot of boiling water, cook the bell peppers and their tops until the peppers are crisp-tender, about 5 minutes. Cool the peppers under cold running water. Coarsely chop the pepper tops.

2. Meanwhile, in a food processor, combine the pork, fennel, and red pepper flakes and process until coarsely chopped. In a large non-stick skillet, heat the oil until hot but not smoking over medium heat. Add the pork mixture and cook, stirring to break up the meat, until the pork is no longer pink, about 3 minutes. Add the broth, wine, scallions, carrots, celery, orange zest, and chopped bell pepper tops and bring to a simmer. Stir in the rice mix and salt, cover, and cook at a bare simmer until the rice is almost tender, about 15 minutes. Remove from the heat and stir in 3 tablespoons of the Parmesan.

3. Preheat the oven to 400°. Spoon the rice mixture into the peppers and place the peppers in an 8-inch square baking dish. Add ¼ inch of water to the pan and cover with foil. Bake for 25 minutes, or until heated through. Divide the peppers among 4 plates, sprinkle the remaining 1 tablespoon Parmesan over, and serve.

Helpful hint: Thick-walled peppers are best for stuffing. If a pepper feels heavy for its size, the flesh should be relatively thick.

Fat: 5g/15%
Calories: 304
Saturated Fat: 1.8g
Carbohydrate: 41g
Protein: 20g
Cholesterol: 41mg
Sodium: 642mg

The fresh Italian-style "sausage" that fills these peppers isn't really sausage, but a mixture you create in your own kitchen from traditional sausage ingredients. It's a blend of pork tenderloin, fennel seeds, and red pepper flakes that's sautéed, then simmered with rice and chopped vegetables to make a tasty stuffing for the peppers. Serve the stuffed peppers on a bed of greens.

OVEN-BARBECUED PORK TENDERLOIN

SERVES: 4
WORKING TIME: 15 MINUTES
TOTAL TIME: 1 HOUR

Both the pork and the sweet potatoes are bathed in an eye-opening sauce made with apple brandy, chili powder, and ginger.

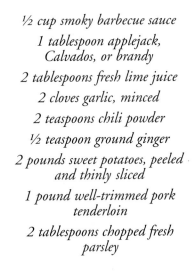

½ cup smoky barbecue sauce

1 tablespoon applejack, Calvados, or brandy

2 tablespoons fresh lime juice

2 cloves garlic, minced

2 teaspoons chili powder

½ teaspoon ground ginger

2 pounds sweet potatoes, peeled and thinly sliced

1 pound well-trimmed pork tenderloin

2 tablespoons chopped fresh parsley

1. Preheat the oven to 425°. Spray a 13 x 9-inch baking pan with nonstick cooking spray.

2. In a small bowl, combine the barbecue sauce, applejack, lime juice, garlic, chili powder, and ginger. Spread the sweet potatoes in the prepared baking pan, spoon two-thirds of the sauce on top, and bake for 15 minutes.

3. Place the pork on top of the sweet potatoes and spoon the remaining sauce over the pork. Roast for 30 minutes, or until the pork is cooked through but still juicy and the potatoes are firm-tender. Transfer the pork to a cutting board and let stand for at least 10 minutes before slicing. Divide the pork and potatoes among 4 plates, sprinkle the potatoes with the parsley, and serve.

Helpful hint: Letting the pork stand before you carve it allows the juices to recede so that they are evenly distributed when you slice the meat. This is true of most roasted meat and poultry.

FAT: 5G/13%
CALORIES: 347
SATURATED FAT: 1.5G
CARBOHYDRATE: 47G
PROTEIN: 27G
CHOLESTEROL: 74MG
SODIUM: 346MG

Beef and Potato Pie

SERVES: 4
WORKING TIME: 35 MINUTES
TOTAL TIME: 1 HOUR

1¾ pounds all-purpose potatoes, peeled and cut into 1-inch cubes

½ cup low-fat (1.5%) buttermilk

¼ cup grated Parmesan cheese

1 egg white, lightly beaten

2 teaspoons olive oil

1 large sweet onion, such as Vidalia, chopped

½ pound green beans, cut into 1-inch lengths

3 cups sliced mushrooms

¾ pound well-trimmed top round of beef, finely diced

2 teaspoons Italian herb seasoning

8-ounce can no-salt-added tomato sauce

2 tablespoons no-salt-added tomato paste

2 tablespoons Worcestershire sauce

¾ teaspoon salt

1. In a medium pot of boiling water, cook the potatoes until firm-tender, about 8 minutes. Drain and transfer to a medium bowl. Add the buttermilk and mash. Stir in the Parmesan and egg white.

2. Preheat the oven to 400°. Spray a 9-inch square baking dish with nonstick cooking spray. Spoon half of the potato mixture into the prepared dish and spread evenly to form a bottom crust.

3. In a large nonstick skillet, heat the oil until hot but not smoking over medium heat. Add the onion, green beans, and mushrooms and cook, stirring frequently, until the onion is tender, about 8 minutes. Add the beef, Italian herb seasoning, tomato sauce, tomato paste, Worcestershire sauce, and salt. Bring to a simmer and cook until the beef is cooked through, about 3 minutes.

4. Spoon the beef mixture over the potato crust. Spoon the remaining potato mixture in a border around the edges of the pan. Bake for 20 to 25 minutes, or until heated through.

Helpful hint: For a dressier crust, you can pipe the mashed potatoes through a pastry tube fitted with a large fluted or star tip.

FAT: 8G/18%
CALORIES: 392
SATURATED FAT: 2.6G
CARBOHYDRATE: 51G
PROTEIN: 31G
CHOLESTEROL: 54MG
SODIUM: 711MG

This shepherd's pie variation partners a tomato-sauced vegetable-beef filling with a topping of Parmesan potatoes.

PORK ENCHILADAS

SERVES: 4
WORKING TIME: 30 MINUTES
TOTAL TIME: 1 HOUR

Pick up a fast-food beef-and-cheese enchilada for dinner and you take on a hefty amount of fat. Our home-cooked pork enchiladas, filled with a saucy mixture of pork and potatoes and topped with Monterey jack cheese, are a considerable improvement. For an even more healthful meal, accompany the enchiladas with a mixed salad.

¾ pound red potatoes, cut into ½-inch cubes

2 teaspoons olive oil

1 red onion, slivered

1 green bell pepper, slivered

½ pound well-trimmed pork tenderloin, cut into ½-inch cubes

1 cup sliced mushrooms

2 cloves garlic, minced

1 tablespoon chili powder

2 teaspoons ground coriander

1 teaspoon dried oregano

16-ounce can no-salt-added tomato purée

2 tablespoons no-salt-added tomato paste

1 tablespoon Worcestershire sauce

¾ teaspoon hot pepper sauce

¾ teaspoon salt

Eight 7-inch corn tortillas

½ cup shredded Monterey jack cheese (2 ounces)

1. In a medium pot of boiling water, cook the potatoes until firm-tender, about 8 minutes. Drain well.

2. Meanwhile, in a large nonstick skillet, heat the oil until hot but not smoking over medium heat. Add the onion and bell pepper and cook, stirring frequently, until the onion is softened, about 5 minutes. Stir in the pork, mushrooms, garlic, chili powder, coriander, and oregano and cook, stirring frequently, until the pork is cooked through, about 5 minutes. Stir in ½ cup of the tomato purée, the tomato paste, Worcestershire sauce, hot pepper sauce, and salt and simmer for 2 minutes to develop the flavors. Remove from the heat and stir in the cooked potatoes.

3. Preheat the oven to 400°. Spray an 11 x 7-inch baking dish with nonstick cooking spray. Brush each tortilla with some of the remaining tomato purée. Dividing evenly, spoon the pork filling down the center of each tortilla and roll up. Place the enchiladas seam-side down in the prepared baking dish, top with the remaining tomato purée, and cover the dish with foil.

4. Bake for 25 to 30 minutes, or until heated through. While the casserole is still hot, sprinkle on the Monterey jack and let sit until melted. Divide among 4 plates and serve.

Helpful hint: Sharp Cheddar could be substituted for the Monterey jack.

FAT: 11G/24%
CALORIES: 416
SATURATED FAT: 3.7G
CARBOHYDRATE: 60G
PROTEIN: 24G
CHOLESTEROL: 52MG
SODIUM: 722MG

L ike an old-fashioned pot pie, this casserole is topped with a complementary crust; but instead of bland pastry dough, the spicy pork filling is covered with neatly fitted wedges of cumin-scented cornmeal. For a touch of color, garnish the finished casserole with chopped cilantro or parsley, if you like.

MEXICAN TAMALE CASSEROLE

SERVES: 4
WORKING TIME: 30 MINUTES
TOTAL TIME: 1 HOUR

1 cup yellow cornmeal

¼ teaspoon salt

1 tablespoon ground cumin

1½ teaspoons dried oregano

1 teaspoon olive oil

1 large green bell pepper, chopped

1 red onion, slivered

2 cloves garlic, minced

1 tablespoon chili powder

⅓ cup chili sauce or ketchup

8-ounce can no-salt-added tomato sauce

1 pickled jalapeño pepper, finely chopped

½ pound well-trimmed pork loin, cut into ½-inch chunks

2 cups frozen corn kernels

¼ cup pitted green olives, chopped

½ cup shredded Cheddar cheese (2 ounces)

1. Preheat the oven to 400°. In a small bowl, combine the cornmeal and 1 cup of cold water. In a large saucepan, bring 1 cup of water, the salt, 1 teaspoon of the cumin, and ½ teaspoon of the oregano to a boil. Add the cornmeal to the boiling water, whisking constantly. Reduce to a simmer and cook, stirring constantly, until the mixture thickens and leaves the sides of the pan, about 5 minutes. Spoon the cornmeal into a 9-inch deep-dish pie plate lined with plastic wrap and shape into a circle (see tip; top photo). Remove the cornmeal (middle photo) and when cool, cut into 8 wedges (bottom photo). Spray the pie plate with nonstick cooking spray.

2. Meanwhile, in a large nonstick skillet, heat the oil until hot but not smoking over medium-high heat. Add the bell pepper, onion, and garlic and cook until the pepper is tender, about 4 minutes. Add the chili powder, chili sauce, tomato sauce, jalapeño, the remaining 2 teaspoons cumin, and remaining 1 teaspoon oregano and cook for 4 minutes to develop the flavors. Stir in the pork, corn, and olives; cover and cook until the pork is cooked through, about 6 minutes. Scrape the mixture into the pie plate and arrange the cornmeal wedges on top.

3. Bake for 25 minutes, or until heated through. Sprinkle the Cheddar over and bake for 5 minutes, or until the cheese is melted. Divide among 4 plates and serve.

FAT: 13G/26%
CALORIES: 443
SATURATED FAT: 4.5G
CARBOHYDRATE: 62G
PROTEIN: 24G
CHOLESTEROL: 48MG
SODIUM: 859MG

LAYERED MEAT LOAF

SERVES: 4
WORKING TIME: 25 MINUTES
TOTAL TIME: 1 HOUR 5 MINUTES

This masterful mosaic boasts layers of ground beef and pork, a spinach-potato mixture, roasted bell peppers, and sweet chili sauce.

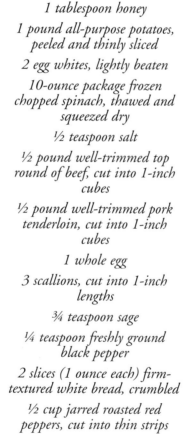

⅓ cup chili sauce

1 tablespoon honey

1 pound all-purpose potatoes, peeled and thinly sliced

2 egg whites, lightly beaten

10-ounce package frozen chopped spinach, thawed and squeezed dry

½ teaspoon salt

½ pound well-trimmed top round of beef, cut into 1-inch cubes

½ pound well-trimmed pork tenderloin, cut into 1-inch cubes

1 whole egg

3 scallions, cut into 1-inch lengths

¾ teaspoon sage

¼ teaspoon freshly ground black pepper

2 slices (1 ounce each) firm-textured white bread, crumbled

½ cup jarred roasted red peppers, cut into thin strips

1. Preheat the oven to 375°. Spray a 9 x 5-inch glass loaf pan with nonstick cooking spray. In a small bowl, combine the chili sauce and honey.

2. In a medium pot of boiling water, cook the potatoes until firm-tender, about 10 minutes. Reserving ⅓ cup of the cooking water, drain the potatoes, place them in a medium bowl, and mash. Set aside to cool slightly, then add the egg whites, spinach, and ¼ teaspoon of the salt, stirring to blend.

3. In a food processor, combine the beef, pork, whole egg, scallions, sage, the remaining ¼ teaspoon salt, and the black pepper. In a small bowl, combine the bread and the reserved potato cooking water. Add the bread mixture to the processor and process with on/off pulses until finely chopped.

4. Spoon half of the chili sauce mixture into the bottom of the prepared loaf pan. Layer half of the beef mixture on top. Spoon in half of the potato mixture and arrange the roasted pepper strips on top. Spoon on the remaining potato mixture. Top with the remaining beef mixture and spread level. Top with the remaining chili sauce mixture and bake for 40 minutes, or until cooked through. Invert the loaf onto a platter, cut into 8 slices, and serve.

FAT: 6G/16%
CALORIES: 341
SATURATED FAT: 1.8G
CARBOHYDRATE: 38G
PROTEIN: 34G
CHOLESTEROL: 123MG
SODIUM: 851MG

ON THE GRILL

4

GRILLED MUSTARD-COATED BEEF

SERVES: 4
WORKING TIME: 15 MINUTES
TOTAL TIME: 30 MINUTES

The light, tangy seasonings rubbed into the flank steak here also flavor the accompanying corn and bean salad. Flank steak (sometimes sold as London broil) is lean and relatively tender, but when broiled or grilled it should not be cooked beyond medium-rare, or it may become tough. Slicing the steak on the diagonal helps enhance its tenderness.

3 tablespoons Dijon mustard
3 tablespoons red wine vinegar
1 teaspoon dried tarragon
¼ teaspoon salt
¾ pound well-trimmed flank steak
2 cloves garlic, minced
1 tablespoon honey
1 cucumber, peeled, halved lengthwise, seeded, and diced
15¼-ounce can red kidney beans, rinsed and drained
2 cups frozen corn kernels, thawed
1 cup cherry tomatoes, quartered
3 scallions, thinly sliced

1. In a medium bowl, combine the mustard, vinegar, tarragon, and salt. Remove 2 tablespoons of the mixture and rub it into the steak along with the garlic. Let the meat stand at room temperature while you make the corn and bean salad and preheat the grill.

2. Preheat the grill to medium heat. Add the honey, cucumber, kidney beans, corn, tomatoes, and scallions to the mustard mixture remaining in the bowl. Refrigerate until serving time.

3. Spray the rack—off the grill—with nonstick cooking spray. Place the steak on the rack, cover, and grill for 7 minutes, or until medium-rare. Let stand for 10 minutes before thinly slicing on the diagonal. Divide the corn and bean salad among 4 plates, place the beef slices alongside, and serve.

Helpful hints: The vegetable mixture can be prepared up to 4 hours in advance; keep it covered in the refrigerator until serving time. The steak may be marinated for several hours or overnight: After rubbing the seasoning mixture and garlic into the steak, put it on a plate, cover with plastic wrap, and refrigerate it until ready to grill.

FAT: 8G/22%
CALORIES: 329
SATURATED FAT: 2.9G
CARBOHYDRATE: 38G
PROTEIN: 26G
CHOLESTEROL: 43MG
SODIUM: 603MG

*T*he combination of grilled steak, bell peppers, and onion brings to mind Mexican fajitas. But instead of wrapping our filling in tortillas, we've piled the citrus-marinated beef and vegetables on toasted Italian bread. If you have a grill topper, you can cook some potatoes alongside the steak, peppers, and onion. Precook the potatoes for 10 minutes before grilling.

Florida Grilled Beef

Serves: 4
Working time: 15 minutes
Total time: 1 hour 10 minutes

3 tablespoons frozen orange juice
concentrate

2 tablespoons fresh lime juice

¾ teaspoon salt

½ teaspoon ground cumin

¼ teaspoon freshly ground black
pepper

¼ teaspoon hot pepper sauce

10 ounces well-trimmed top
round of beef, in one piece

1 red onion, cut into thick
rounds

2 red bell peppers, quartered
lengthwise and seeded

1 green bell pepper, quartered
lengthwise and seeded

4 ounces Italian bread, halved
crosswise, then horizontally

1 tablespoon olive oil

8 tomato slices

1. In a medium bowl, combine the orange juice concentrate, lime juice, ¼ teaspoon of the salt, the cumin, black pepper, and hot pepper sauce. Add the beef and onion, turning to coat. Set aside to marinate for 30 minutes at room temperature.

2. Preheat the grill (with a grill topper, if possible; see tip) to medium heat. Spray the rack (and grill topper)—off the grill—with non-stick cooking spray. Reserving the marinade, place the meat on the rack, cover, and grill for 3 minutes. Place the onion and bell peppers, skin-sides down, on the grill topper, re-cover, and grill, turning and basting the beef and onion with some of the reserved marinade, for 7 minutes, or until the beef is medium-rare, the peppers are charred, and the onion is crisp-tender. Place the bread, cut-sides down, on the grill and cook until lightly browned, about 30 seconds.

3. Let the beef stand for 10 minutes before thinly slicing on the diagonal. When cool enough to handle, peel the peppers and cut into ½-inch-wide strips. In a medium bowl, toss together the peppers, onion, oil, and the remaining ½ teaspoon salt. Divide the bread among 4 plates, top with the tomato slices, sliced beef, and the onion-pepper mixture, and serve.

Helpful hint: The beef can be marinated in a covered dish in the refrigerator for up to 8 hours.

Fat: 7g/24%
Calories: 264
Saturated Fat: 1.6g
Carbohydrate: 29g
Protein: 21g
Cholesterol: 45mg
Sodium: 626mg

TIP

To make your own grill topper, tear off a large piece of heavy-duty foil and fold it in half to make a double layer. Using a two-tined fork, make a series of holes over the entire surface of the foil. Use the punctured foil to cover the grill rack—before preheating—and proceed as directed.

The Southeast Asian satay (or saté) is usually made with strips or chunks of meat (beef, lamb, pork, or chicken). We've created an innovative satay from ground pork blended with garlic, ketchup, scallions, and ginger. After grilling, the satay is served on a bed of rice, with a delicate peanut sauce and a refreshingly minty cucumber-tomato relish.

Grilled Pork Satay

SERVES: 4
WORKING TIME: 20 MINUTES
TOTAL TIME: 35 MINUTES

2 tablespoons plus 1 teaspoon
rice vinegar

2¼ teaspoons sugar

½ teaspoon red pepper flakes

1 teaspoon salt

1 large cucumber, peeled, halved
lengthwise, seeded, and cut into
¼-inch dice

1 tomato, cut into ¼-inch dice

3 tablespoons chopped fresh mint
or basil

1 cup long-grain rice

2 tablespoons reduced-sodium
chicken broth, defatted

5 teaspoons smooth peanut
butter

1 pound well-trimmed pork
tenderloin, cut into chunks

3 cloves garlic, peeled

2 slices (1 ounce each) firm-
textured white bread, crumbled

2 tablespoons low-fat (1%) milk

¼ cup ketchup

4 scallions, thinly sliced

¾ teaspoon ground ginger

1. In a medium bowl, combine 2 tablespoons of the vinegar, 2 tea-spoons of the sugar, the red pepper flakes, and ¼ teaspoon of the salt. Add the cucumber, tomato, and mint and toss to combine. Refrigerate the cucumber relish until serving time. In a medium saucepan, bring 2¼ cups of water to a boil. Add the rice and ¼ teaspoon of the salt, reduce to a simmer, cover, and cook until the rice is tender, about 17 minutes.

2. Meanwhile, preheat the grill (with a grill topper, if possible) to medium heat. In a food processor, combine the broth, peanut but-ter, the remaining 1 teaspoon vinegar, and remaining ¼ teaspoon sugar and process until smooth. Transfer the sauce to a small bowl. In the same processor bowl, combine the meat and garlic and process until finely ground. Transfer to a medium bowl and stir in the bread, milk, ketchup, scallions, ginger, and the remaining ½ teaspoon salt. Shape the mixture into 8 log shapes (see tip; top photo). Skewer each log onto two 8-inch-skewers (bottom photo).

3. Spray the rack (or grill topper)—off the grill—with nonstick cook-ing spray. Place the skewers on the rack, cover, and grill, turning once, for 7 minutes, or until the pork is browned and cooked through. Divide the rice among 4 plates and spoon the cucumber relish alongside. Top the rice with two pork skewers and the peanut sauce and serve.

FAT: 10G/20%
CALORIES: 460
SATURATED FAT: 2.7G
CARBOHYDRATE: 58G
PROTEIN: 34G
CHOLESTEROL: 81MG
SODIUM: 924MG

Divide the pork mixture into eight portions and shape each one into a thick little log-shaped patty. Insert two wooden skewers lengthwise into the end of each patty.

PORK BURGERS WITH SWEET POTATO RELISH

SERVES: 4
WORKING TIME: 20 MINUTES
TOTAL TIME: 30 MINUTES

8 ounces sweet potato, peeled and cut into ½-inch cubes

½ cup frozen corn kernels, thawed

1 tomato, coarsely chopped

⅓ cup plus 2 tablespoons chili sauce

2 scallions, thinly sliced

2 tablespoons red wine vinegar

1 teaspoon olive oil

1¼ pounds well-trimmed pork tenderloin, cut into chunks

2 slices (1 ounce each) firm-textured white bread, crumbled

½ cup seltzer or club soda

2 tablespoons chopped pickled jalapeño pepper

¾ teaspoon freshly ground black pepper

¼ teaspoon dried sage

4 hamburger buns

1. In a medium pot of boiling water, cook the sweet potato until firm-tender, about 7 minutes. Drain well. Transfer to a medium bowl and add the corn, tomato, 2 tablespoons of the chili sauce, the scallions, vinegar, and oil. Toss to combine and refrigerate until serving time.

2. Meanwhile, in a food processor, process the pork until finely ground. Transfer the pork to a large bowl and stir in the bread, seltzer, jalapeño, black pepper, sage, and the remaining ⅓ cup chili sauce. Shape the mixture into 4 patties.

3. Preheat the grill to medium heat. Spray the rack—off the grill—with nonstick cooking spray. Place the burgers on the rack, cover, and grill, turning once, for 8 minutes, or until cooked through but still juicy. Place the buns, cut-sides down, on the grill and cook until lightly browned and toasted, about 30 seconds.

4. Divide the buns among 4 plates, top with the burgers and relish, and serve.

Helpful hint: The chilied sweet potato relish would be equally delicious on turkey burgers or sliced turkey sandwiches.

FAT: 11G/21%
CALORIES: 475
SATURATED FAT: 3.2G
CARBOHYDRATE: 53G
PROTEIN: 40G
CHOLESTEROL: 100MG
SODIUM: 883MG

Move over, turkey burger—here's another contender for the title of "leanest, juiciest burger." Here, we've ground pork tenderloin and combined it with fresh crumbled bread and seltzer—a tried-and-true "secret ingredient" for tender burgers and meatballs. Serve the burgers on toasted buns, topped with the chunky sweet potato relish and accompanied by a summery salad.

When
you see the word
diablo or diable
(meaning devil) in a
recipe title, get ready
for a burst of peppery
flavor. Our tomato-
based diablo sauce is
spiked with red-hot
cayenne. The grilled
beef rolls hide sliced
prosciutto and herbs.
They're cooked
alongside skewers of
sweet potatoes,
mushrooms, and onion.

Skewered Beef Rolls with Sauce Diablo

Serves: 4
Working time: 25 minutes
Total time: 35 minutes

1½ pounds sweet potatoes, peeled and cut into 24 chunks

½ cup reduced-sodium chicken broth, defatted

1 onion, cut into 16 chunks

8 large mushroom caps, halved

1 cup canned crushed tomatoes

4 scallions, thinly sliced

1½ teaspoons Worcestershire sauce

¼ teaspoon cayenne pepper

1 teaspoon grated lemon zest

½ teaspoon salt

½ teaspoon dried rosemary, crumbled

½ teaspoon dried thyme

10 ounces well-trimmed beef sirloin, cut into 8 slices and pounded (see page 8) ⅛ inch thick

2 ounces thinly sliced prosciutto or baked ham, cut into 8 pieces

1. In a large saucepan of boiling water, cook the sweet potatoes until firm-tender, about 12 minutes. Drain well and transfer to a large bowl. Add all but 2 tablespoons of the broth, the onion, and mushrooms, tossing to coat. In a medium bowl, combine the tomatoes, scallions, Worcestershire sauce, cayenne, and ¼ teaspoon of the lemon zest. Measure out ¼ cup of the diablo sauce, transfer to a small bowl, and stir in the remaining 2 tablespoons broth; set aside to use as a baste.

2. In a small bowl, combine the salt, rosemary, thyme, and the remaining ¾ teaspoon lemon zest. Sprinkle the mixture over the beef slices. Place a piece of prosciutto on top of each beef slice (see tip; top photo) and roll up from one short end (middle photo). Thread each beef roll onto two 8-inch skewers (bottom photo).

3. Preheat the grill to medium heat. Alternately thread the mushrooms, onion, and sweet potatoes onto eight 10-inch skewers. Spray the rack—off the grill—with nonstick cooking spray. Place the skewers on the rack, brush the beef rolls with the tomato baste, cover, and grill, turning once, for 7 minutes, or until the beef rolls are just cooked through and the vegetables are tender. Divide the beef rolls and vegetables among 4 plates. Top with the reserved diablo sauce and serve.

Helpful hint: Prosciutto is Italian unsmoked, salt-cured ham.

Fat: 7g/20%
Calories: 314
Saturated Fat: 2.1g
Carbohydrate: 40g
Protein: 25g
Cholesterol: 59mg
Sodium: 781mg

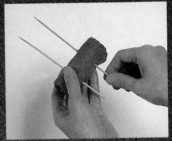

Mexican Flank Steak with Rice and Bean Salad

SERVES: 4
WORKING TIME: 15 MINUTES
TOTAL TIME: 25 MINUTES

Most Mexican restaurant meals come with "sides" of rice and beans. These extra carbohydrates improve the nutrient balance, but unfortunately the beans are usually fried in fat. Our lightened interpretation is a mixture of rice and pinto beans, tossed with fresh tomato, salsa, and fragrant herbs. The warm rice-and-bean salad accompanies salsa-marinated flank steak.

1 cup long-grain rice
½ teaspoon salt
19-ounce can pinto beans, rinsed and drained
1 tomato, coarsely chopped
¼ cup chopped fresh cilantro or basil
¼ cup plus 2 tablespoons mild to medium-hot prepared salsa
2 tablespoons fresh lime juice
1 teaspoon olive oil
1 pound well-trimmed flank steak
Four 6-inch flour tortillas

1. In a medium saucepan, bring 2¼ cups of water to a boil. Add the rice and ¼ teaspoon of the salt, reduce to a simmer, cover, and cook until the rice is tender, about 17 minutes.

2. Meanwhile, in a medium bowl, combine the remaining ¼ teaspoon salt, the beans, tomato, cilantro, and 2 tablespoons of the salsa. In another medium bowl, combine the remaining ¼ cup salsa, the lime juice, and oil. Add the flank steak and let stand while you preheat the grill.

3. Preheat the grill to medium heat. Spray the rack—off the grill—with nonstick cooking spray. Reserving the marinade, place the steak on the rack, cover, and grill, turning once and basting with some of the reserved marinade, for 7 minutes, or until medium-rare. Let the steak stand for 10 minutes before thinly slicing on the diagonal. In a large bowl, combine the rice and beans.

4. Place the tortillas on the grill for 30 seconds, turning once, to warm them. Divide the rice and bean mixture among 4 plates and place the beef slices alongside. Serve with the tortillas on the side.

Helpful hint: You can use red beans, kidney beans, or black beans in place of the pinto beans, if you like.

FAT: 12G/21%
CALORIES: 511
SATURATED FAT: 4.2G
CARBOHYDRATE: 64G
PROTEIN: 33G
CHOLESTEROL: 57MG
SODIUM: 768MG

GREEK-STYLE BEEF IN PITAS

SERVES: 4
WORKING TIME: 25 MINUTES
TOTAL TIME: 35 MINUTES

These overstuffed pitas are filled with garlicky grilled beef strips, chopped vegetable salad, and a minty yogurt sauce.

½ teaspoon grated lemon zest

3 tablespoons fresh lemon juice

2 cloves garlic, minced

¾ teaspoon dried oregano

½ teaspoon salt

½ teaspoon freshly ground black pepper

¾ pound well-trimmed beef sirloin

1 green bell pepper, cut into ¼-inch dice

1 tomato, coarsely chopped

1 cucumber, peeled, halved lengthwise, seeded, and cut into ¼-inch dice

½ cup chopped fresh mint

½ teaspoon hot pepper sauce

½ cup plain nonfat yogurt

Four 8-inch pita breads, tops cut open

1. In a small bowl, with the back of a spoon, mash together the lemon zest, 2 tablespoons of the lemon juice, the garlic, oregano, ¼ teaspoon of the salt, and the black pepper. Rub the mixture onto the beef and let stand while you make the minted vegetable mixture and preheat the grill.

2. Preheat the grill to medium heat. In a medium bowl, combine the bell pepper, tomato, cucumber, ¼ cup of the mint, the hot pepper sauce, the remaining 1 tablespoon lemon juice, and remaining ¼ teaspoon salt. In a small bowl, combine the yogurt and the remaining ¼ cup mint; refrigerate until serving time.

3. Spray the rack—off the grill—with nonstick cooking spray. Place the beef on the rack, cover, and grill, turning once, for 7 minutes, or until medium-rare. Grill the pitas until lightly toasted, about 30 seconds. Let the beef stand for 10 minutes before thinly slicing.

4. Add the beef to the minted vegetable mixture, tossing to combine. Spoon the meat and vegetable mixture into the pitas, divide among 4 plates, spoon the mint sauce over, and serve.

Helpful hint: You can prepare the recipe through the end of step 2 up to 4 hours in advance; keep the beef covered in the refrigerator until ready to grill.

FAT: 6G/14%
CALORIES: 401
SATURATED FAT: 2G
CARBOHYDRATE: 56G
PROTEIN: 30G
CHOLESTEROL: 57MG
SODIUM: 816MG

Grilled Beef Teriyaki

SERVES: 4
WORKING TIME: 10 MINUTES
TOTAL TIME: 40 MINUTES

¼ cup reduced-sodium chicken broth, defatted

3 tablespoons reduced-sodium soy sauce

2 tablespoons rice vinegar

4 teaspoons firmly packed dark brown sugar

½ teaspoon ground ginger

½ teaspoon salt

¾ pound well-trimmed top round of beef

2 sweet onions, such as Vidalia, cut into ½-inch-thick rounds

4 plum tomatoes, halved lengthwise

1 cup long-grain rice

1. In a medium bowl, make the teriyaki sauce: Combine the broth, soy sauce, vinegar, brown sugar, ginger, and ¼ teaspoon of the salt. Measure out ¼ cup of the sauce and set aside. Add the beef, onions, and tomatoes to the mixture remaining in the bowl, tossing gently to coat. Set aside to marinate for 30 minutes.

2. In a medium saucepan, bring 2¼ cups of water to a boil. Add the rice and the remaining ¼ teaspoon salt, reduce to a simmer, cover, and cook until the rice is tender, about 17 minutes.

3. Meanwhile, preheat the grill (with a grill topper, if possible) to medium heat. Spray the rack (and grill topper)—off the grill—with nonstick cooking spray. Place the beef on the rack and place the onions and tomatoes on the grill topper. Cover and grill, turning several times, for 7 minutes, or until the beef is medium-rare and the onions are lightly browned and crisp-tender and the tomatoes have collapsed slightly. Let the beef stand for 10 minutes before thinly slicing.

4. Divide the rice among 4 plates. Place the sliced beef, onions, and tomatoes alongside, spoon the reserved teriyaki sauce over, and serve.

Helpful hint: Vidalia onions, grown in Georgia, are sweet and mild enough to eat raw. Maui and Walla Walla onions can be substituted.

FAT: 7G/15%
CALORIES: 411
SATURATED FAT: 2.4G
CARBOHYDRATE: 61G
PROTEIN: 27G
CHOLESTEROL: 54MG
SODIUM: 822MG

Pungent yet sweet, teriyaki sauce makes an irresistible glaze for beef, onions, and tomatoes.

115

GRILLED PORK WITH PEACH CHUTNEY

SERVES: 4
WORKING TIME: 15 MINUTES
TOTAL TIME: 50 MINUTES

As pleasant as applesauce is with roast pork, our colorful peach chutney holds far more fascination. The peach slices (we use frozen, but you could use fresh), along with chunks of onion and red bell pepper, are simmered in a mixture of wine vinegar, sugar, ginger, nutmeg, cloves, and pepper. The chutney serves as a sauce for slices of spice-rubbed grilled pork tenderloin.

1 red bell pepper, cut into ½-inch squares
1 onion, cut into ½-inch chunks
¼ cup sugar
3 tablespoons red wine vinegar
1 teaspoon ground ginger
½ teaspoon salt
¼ teaspoon freshly ground black pepper
⅛ teaspoon nutmeg
⅛ teaspoon ground cloves
3 cups frozen or fresh peach slices
2 teaspoons paprika
¾ pound well-trimmed pork tenderloin, cut into 4 pieces

1. In a medium saucepan, combine the bell pepper, onion, sugar, vinegar, ½ teaspoon of the ginger, ¼ teaspoon of the salt, the black pepper, nutmeg, and cloves. Bring to a boil over medium heat, reduce to a simmer, and cook until the bell pepper is crisp-tender, about 10 minutes. Add the peaches and cook until the chutney is richly flavored and of a jam-like consistency, about 15 minutes. Cool to room temperature.

2. Preheat the grill to medium heat. In a small bowl, combine the paprika, the remaining ½ teaspoon ginger, and remaining ¼ teaspoon salt. Rub the mixture into the pork.

3. Spray the rack—off the grill—with nonstick cooking spray. Place the pork on the rack, cover, and grill, turning once, for 8 minutes, or until cooked through but still juicy. Let the pork stand for 10 minutes before thinly slicing. Spoon the chutney onto 4 plates, place the pork alongside, and serve.

Helpful hint: The chutney may be prepared several days in advance and kept refrigerated until serving time. It can be served at room temperature or chilled.

FAT: 4G/14%
CALORIES: 251
SATURATED FAT: 1.5G
CARBOHYDRATE: 33G
PROTEIN: 21G
CHOLESTEROL: 60MG
SODIUM: 317MG

What in some parts of the country is called a "sub" is elsewhere known as a hero, grinder, hoagie, or po' boy. These oversized sandwiches, stuffed with meat and vegetables, are satisfying meals in themselves. Ours is filled with sage-scented pork loin and a tangy apple relish. Serve the subs with carrot-and-cabbage slaw and some pickle slices.

Grilled Pork Subs

SERVES: 4
WORKING TIME: 15 MINUTES
TOTAL TIME: 35 MINUTES

2 tablespoons reduced-fat mayonnaise

3 tablespoons frozen apple juice concentrate, thawed

1 tablespoon cider vinegar

½ teaspoon salt

2 green apples, such as Granny Smith, cored and cut into ¼-inch dice

1 red apple, such as McIntosh or Rome Beauty, cored and cut into ¼-inch dice

½ cup raisins

½ cup diced red onion

¾ pound well-trimmed center-cut pork loin, in one piece

½ teaspoon freshly ground black pepper

¼ teaspoon dried sage

Four 2-ounce rolls, split

1 cup torn lettuce leaves

1. Place the mayonnaise in a medium bowl. Whisk in the apple juice concentrate, 1 tablespoon at a time. Whisk in the vinegar and ¼ teaspoon of the salt. Stir in the apples, raisins, and red onion, tossing to combine. Refrigerate until ready to use.

2. Preheat the grill to medium heat. Butterfly the pork loin (see tip) and rub the pepper, sage, and the remaining ¼ teaspoon salt onto it.

3. Spray the rack—off the grill—with nonstick cooking spray. Place the pork on the rack, cover, and grill, turning once, for 15 minutes, or until lightly browned and cooked through but still juicy. Let the pork stand for 10 minutes before thinly slicing. Grill the rolls, cut-sides down, until lightly toasted, about 30 seconds.

4. Divide the rolls among 4 plates, top with the lettuce, pork, and apple relish and serve.

Helpful hint: The green apples provide a colorful contrast to the red onion in the relish. Other varieties you can try include Newtown Pippins, Crispin (formerly called Mutsu), and Rhode Island Greenings.

TIP

To butterfly the pork loin, use a sharp knife and carefully slice it from one edge, stopping just short of cutting all the way through. Then open up the two halves like a book.

FAT: 9G/18%
CALORIES: 451
SATURATED FAT: 2.7G
CARBOHYDRATE: 68G
PROTEIN: 26G
CHOLESTEROL: 52MG
SODIUM: 712MG

Tandoori Pork Kebabs

SERVES: 4
WORKING TIME: 25 MINUTES
TOTAL TIME: 25 MINUTES PLUS MARINATING TIME

1 cup plain nonfat yogurt

2 cloves garlic, minced

4 teaspoons chopped fresh ginger

¾ teaspoon chili powder

¾ teaspoon salt

½ teaspoon turmeric

½ teaspoon ground cumin

10 ounces well-trimmed pork tenderloin, cut into 16 chunks

1 onion, cut into 1-inch chunks

16 cherry tomatoes

16 canned juice-packed pineapple chunks, juice reserved

1 cup couscous

2 cups boiling water

1. In a large bowl, combine the yogurt, garlic, ginger, chili powder, ½ teaspoon of the salt, the turmeric, and cumin. Measure out ½ cup of the yogurt mixture and set aside to use as a sauce. Add the pork, onion, tomatoes, and pineapple to the mixture remaining in the bowl, tossing to coat. Marinate for at least 30 minutes or up to overnight.

2. Preheat the grill to medium heat. Alternately thread the pork, onion, tomatoes, and pineapple onto eight 8-inch skewers.

3. In a medium bowl, combine the couscous, boiling water, and the remaining ¼ teaspoon salt. Stir well, cover, and let stand until the couscous has softened, about 5 minutes.

4. Spray the rack—off the grill—with nonstick cooking spray. Place the skewers on the rack, cover, and grill, turning once, for 8 minutes, or until the pork is cooked through but still juicy and the vegetables are firm-tender. Stir 2 tablespoons of the reserved pineapple juice into the yogurt sauce. Spoon the couscous onto a platter, top with the skewers, and serve the yogurt sauce on the side.

Helpful hint: The kebabs would be equally good served on a bed of rice (plain or cooked in broth).

FAT: 4G/10%
CALORIES: 353
SATURATED FAT: 1.4G
CARBOHYDRATE: 51G
PROTEIN: 27G
CHOLESTEROL: 51MG
SODIUM: 505MG

A hot grill makes a good substitute for a brick-and-clay tandoor—an Indian oven that can be heated to over 500 degrees. Foods to be cooked in a tandoor are usually marinated in a yogurt mixture. Our kebabs feature chunks of pork alternating with pineapple, onion, and cherry tomatoes. The turmeric and cumin in the marinade give the kebabs a golden finish.

FLANK STEAK WITH SPICED PINEAPPLE RELISH

SERVES: 4
WORKING TIME: 20 MINUTES
TOTAL TIME: 40 MINUTES

You get more than great flavor when you prepare this tropical relish. In addition to being a tart-sweet complement to the grilled beef, the acidity of the pineapple helps tenderize the meat. The flank steak is marinated in pineapple purée before cooking, then served with a chunky pineapple relish. Add a leafy salad and you've got a great meal.

20-ounce can juice-packed pineapple chunks, drained, juice reserved

3 tablespoons honey

2 tablespoons grated fresh ginger

2 tablespoons reduced-sodium soy sauce

2 scallions, coarsely chopped

1 clove garlic, peeled

½ teaspoon salt

¾ pound well-trimmed flank steak

1 red bell pepper, cut into ¼-inch dice

½ red onion, cut into ¼-inch dice

½ teaspoon freshly ground black pepper

⅛ teaspoon ground allspice

1. In a food processor, combine ½ cup of the pineapple chunks, 3 tablespoons of the reserved pineapple juice, 1 tablespoon of the honey, the ginger, 1 tablespoon of the soy sauce, the scallions, garlic, and salt. Process until smooth. Measure out ¼ cup of the mixture, place in a medium bowl, and set aside. Brush the flank steak with the remaining pineapple purée and let marinate at room temperature for 20 minutes.

2. Meanwhile, preheat the grill to medium heat. Add the bell pepper, onion, black pepper, allspice, the remaining pineapple chunks, the remaining 2 tablespoons honey, the remaining 1 tablespoon soy sauce, and 3 tablespoons of the reserved pineapple juice to the pineapple purée in the medium bowl.

3. Spray the rack—off the grill—with nonstick cooking spray. Reserving the marinade, place the steak on the grill, cover, and grill, turning once and basting with the reserved marinade, for 7 minutes, or until medium-rare. Let stand for 10 minutes before slicing. Divide the pineapple relish among 4 plates, place the steak slices alongside, and serve.

Helpful hint: You can marinate the steak for up to 8 hours, but it should be covered and refrigerated if you do so.

FAT: 7G/22%
CALORIES: 290
SATURATED FAT: 2.8G
CARBOHYDRATE: 41G
PROTEIN: 19G
CHOLESTEROL: 43MG
SODIUM: 633MG

This
is the sort of barbecue
sandwich you might
find in the South. It's
made with pork that's
been basted with a
peppery vinegar
marinade, pulled into
shreds after cooking,
and then combined
with a ketchup-based
sauce and served on a
bun. We've topped the
meat with tender
grilled onions. A bean
salad, dressed with a
light vinaigrette, makes
a great side dish.

SOUTHERN BARBECUE SANDWICHES

SERVES: 4
WORKING TIME: 20 MINUTES
TOTAL TIME: 1 HOUR

½ cup cider vinegar

2 tablespoons firmly packed light or dark brown sugar

1 tablespoon molasses

¼ teaspoon salt

¼ teaspoon freshly ground black pepper

¼ teaspoon red pepper flakes

10 ounces well-trimmed pork tenderloin

½ cup orange juice

2 tablespoons ketchup

2 teaspoons olive oil

3 red onions, sliced into thick rings

4 hamburger buns

1. In a small saucepan, combine the vinegar, 4 teaspoons of the brown sugar, the molasses, salt, black pepper, and red pepper flakes. Bring to a boil and cook, stirring, until the sugar dissolves, about 1 minute. Pour half of the mixture into a large bowl, add the pork, and marinate for 30 minutes. Set the remaining mixture aside. Meanwhile, preheat the grill (with a grill topper, if possible) to medium heat. In a medium bowl, combine the orange juice, ketchup, the remaining 2 teaspoons brown sugar, and the oil. Add the onions, tossing to coat.

2. Spray the rack (and grill topper)—off the grill—with nonstick cooking spray. Reserving the marinade, place the pork on the rack, cover, and grill for 10 minutes, turning and basting every 5 minutes with the marinade. Reserving the marinade, place the onions on the grill topper. Grill the pork and onions for 10 minutes, turning and basting the pork and turning the onions, until the onions are lightly browned and the pork is cooked through. Place the hamburger buns, cut-sides down, on the grill and grill until lightly toasted, about 30 seconds.

3. Shred the pork (see tip) and, in a large bowl, combine the pork and the reserved vinegar mixture. Coarsely chop the onions and toss with the reserved onion marinade. Divide the buns among 4 plates, top with the shredded pork and the onion relish, and serve.

FAT: 8G/20%
CALORIES: 360
SATURATED FAT: 2G
CARBOHYDRATE: 51G
PROTEIN: 22G
CHOLESTEROL: 50MG
SODIUM: 518MG

After grilling, the pork will separate easily into shreds: When it's cool enough to handle, use your fingers to pull it apart along the grain of the meat.

HERBED BEEF KEBABS

SERVES: 4
WORKING TIME: 15 MINUTES
TOTAL TIME: 30 MINUTES

Kebabs are easy to grill and, if you use handsome skewers like these, very impressive to serve as well. Note that the skewers have flat (rather than round) blades to help keep the food from slipping and twisting as it grills. For these kebabs, the steak, squash, potatoes, and tomatoes are bathed in a pesto-like marinade. Serve a tossed green salad alongside.

1½ pounds red potatoes, cut into 16 wedges

1¼ cups reduced-sodium chicken broth, defatted

1 tablespoon olive oil

⅔ cup packed fresh basil leaves

3 cloves garlic, peeled

¾ teaspoon salt

¾ pound well-trimmed beef sirloin, cut into 16 chunks

1 zucchini, halved lengthwise and cut crosswise into 16 pieces

1 yellow summer squash, halved lengthwise and cut crosswise into 16 pieces

16 cherry tomatoes

1. In a medium pot of boiling water, cook the potatoes until firm-tender, about 10 minutes. Drain well.

2. Meanwhile, in a food processor, combine the broth, oil, basil, garlic, and salt and process until smooth. Transfer the mixture to a large bowl and add the beef, zucchini, yellow squash, tomatoes, and the potatoes, tossing to coat.

3. Preheat the grill to medium heat. Reserving the marinade, alternately thread the beef, zucchini, yellow squash, tomatoes, and potatoes onto 8 skewers.

4. Spray the rack—off the grill—with nonstick cooking spray. Place the skewers on the rack, cover, and grill, turning and basting the skewers with the reserved marinade, for 7 minutes, or until the potatoes are golden brown and the beef is medium-rare.

Helpful hint: You can marinate the beef and vegetables up to 2 hours in advance; cover the bowl and place it in the refrigerator.

FAT: 9G/25%
CALORIES: 329
SATURATED FAT: 2.3G
CARBOHYDRATE: 37G
PROTEIN: 26G
CHOLESTEROL: 57MG
SODIUM: 650MG

GRILLED PORK CHOP DINNER

SERVES: 4
WORKING TIME: 20 MINUTES
TOTAL TIME: 50 MINUTES

This winning dinner doesn't really take very long to make. Some of the total time is actually free time for the cook—while the pork chops marinate, the corn soaks in water (to keep it moist), and the coleslaw mellows. Once the chops and corn go on the grill, it's a matter of minutes until the meal is ready. Serve corn bread or warm biscuits to sop up the extra sauce.

4 ears of corn, in their husks
¾ teaspoon chili powder
¼ teaspoon ground ginger
⅛ teaspoon ground allspice
2½ teaspoons sugar
½ teaspoon salt
Four 6-ounce center-cut pork chops
¼ cup plain nonfat yogurt
2 tablespoons cider vinegar
1 tablespoon reduced-fat mayonnaise
½ teaspoon freshly ground black pepper
4 cups shredded cabbage
4 scallions, thinly sliced
1 red bell pepper, cut into 2 x ¼-inch strips
½ cup barbecue sauce
2 tablespoons fresh lime juice

1. Place the unhusked corn in a large pot of water and set aside to soak for 30 minutes. In a small bowl, combine the chili powder, ginger, allspice, ½ teaspoon of the sugar, and ¼ teaspoon of the salt. Rub the mixture into both sides of the pork chops. Let stand for 30 minutes.

2. Meanwhile, in a medium bowl, combine the yogurt, vinegar, mayonnaise, the remaining 2 teaspoons sugar, remaining ¼ teaspoon salt, and the black pepper. Add the cabbage, scallions, and bell pepper and toss to combine. Refrigerate until serving time.

3. Preheat the grill to medium heat. Spray the rack—off the grill—with nonstick cooking spray. Place the unhusked corn on the rack. Add the pork chops and brush them with 2 tablespoons of the barbecue sauce. Cover and grill, turning the pork once and brushing with another 2 tablespoons of the barbecue sauce, for 12 minutes, or until the corn is heated through and the pork chops are browned and cooked through.

4. Husk the corn and sprinkle with the lime juice. Divide the corn among 4 plates and place the chops and coleslaw alongside. Brush the chops with the remaining barbecue sauce and serve.

Helpful hint: There's no need to remove the silk from the corn. After grilling, the silk will slip off when the husks are removed.

FAT: 12G/28%
CALORIES: 388
SATURATED FAT: 3.7G
CARBOHYDRATE: 33G
PROTEIN: 40G
CHOLESTEROL: 92MG
SODIUM: 670MG

ALL-AMERICAN BEEF BURGERS

SERVES: 4
WORKING TIME: 15 MINUTES
TOTAL TIME: 25 MINUTES

Seek no further for the perfect beef burger: This one's lean, moist, subtly spicy, and topped with a creamy ketchup sauce.

¾ pound well-trimmed top round of beef, cut into chunks

2 slices (1 ounce each) firm-textured white bread, crumbled

¼ cup low-fat (1%) milk

1 onion, finely chopped

½ cup snipped fresh dill

2 tablespoons Dijon mustard

1 tablespoon capers, rinsed and drained

¼ teaspoon salt

¼ teaspoon freshly ground black pepper

2 tablespoons reduced-fat sour cream

2 tablespoons plain nonfat yogurt

2 tablespoons ketchup

4 hard rolls, split

4 green leaf lettuce leaves

4 red onion slices

8 tomato slices

1. Preheat the grill to medium heat. In a food processor, process the beef until finely ground. Transfer to a medium bowl and stir in the bread, milk, onion, 6 tablespoons of the dill, the mustard, capers, salt, and pepper. Shape the mixture into 4 burgers.

2. In a small bowl, combine the sour cream, yogurt, ketchup, and the remaining 2 tablespoons dill.

3. Spray the rack—off the grill—with nonstick cooking spray. Place the burgers on the rack, cover, and grill, turning once, for 5 minutes, or until medium-rare. Grill the rolls, cut-sides down, until lightly toasted, about 30 seconds. Divide the rolls among 4 plates. Place a leaf of lettuce and burger on each roll, top with an onion slice, 2 tomato slices, and some of the sour cream-ketchup mixture, and serve.

Helpful hint: These burgers would be great served on toasted onion rolls instead of plain hard rolls.

FAT: 8G/18%
CALORIES: 391
SATURATED FAT: 2.1G
CARBOHYDRATE: 48G
PROTEIN: 30G
CHOLESTEROL: 57MG
SODIUM: 950MG

SALADS

5

Beef and Orzo Salad

SERVES: 4
WORKING TIME: 15 MINUTES
TOTAL TIME: 30 MINUTES

Bring your heartiest appetite to the table, and this salad will satisfy it. While low in fat, the dish is no lightweight: Pasta and sirloin steak are its two main components, with broccoli, bell pepper, and greens adding textural variety as well as admirable nutritional value. The dressing is a balsamic vinaigrette seasoned with the same herbs that flavor the beef.

¼ teaspoon freshly ground black pepper

½ teaspoon salt

½ teaspoon dried rosemary, crumbled

½ teaspoon dried thyme

10 ounces well-trimmed beef sirloin

8 ounces orzo pasta

4 cups broccoli florets

¼ cup balsamic or red wine vinegar

4 teaspoons olive oil

2 scallions, thinly sliced

1 red bell pepper, cut into ½-inch squares

6 cups mixed torn greens

1. Preheat the broiler. In a small bowl, combine the black pepper, ¼ teaspoon of the salt, ¼ teaspoon of the rosemary, and ¼ teaspoon of the thyme. Rub the beef with the herb mixture and broil for about 3½ minutes per side, or until medium-rare. Place the beef on a plate and let it stand for 10 minutes. Thinly slice the beef on the diagonal, then cut it into bite-size pieces, reserving any juices on the plate.

2. Meanwhile, in a large pot of boiling water, cook the orzo until just tender. Add the broccoli during the last 2 minutes of cooking time. Drain well.

3. In a large bowl, combine the beef juices, vinegar, oil, the remaining ¼ teaspoon salt, remaining ¼ teaspoon rosemary, and remaining ¼ teaspoon thyme. Stir in the beef, orzo, broccoli, scallions, bell pepper, and greens, tossing to combine. Serve warm, at room temperature, or chilled.

Helpful hints: This salad calls for sturdy greens, such as romaine, escarole, radicchio, or curly chicory. If you want to serve the salad chilled, do not add the greens until just before serving.

FAT: 10G/21%
CALORIES: 420
SATURATED FAT: 2.3G
CARBOHYDRATE: 54G
PROTEIN: 30G
CHOLESTEROL: 47MG
SODIUM: 392MG

PORK TACO SALAD

SERVES: 4
WORKING TIME: 15 MINUTES
TOTAL TIME: 45 MINUTES

The puffed tortilla shell that usually crowns a taco salad is by far the fattiest part of the dish. Deep-fried, it can account for as much as 30 grams of fat! But with baked tortilla chips, you can serve a tasty salad, replete with pork, beans, and plenty of chips, and still keep the total fat down to 7 grams. Green peas combined with avocado make a lower-fat guacamole layer for the salad.

½ pound well-trimmed pork tenderloin
1 teaspoon ground cumin
1 teaspoon chili powder
½ teaspoon salt
¾ cup frozen peas, thawed
½ cup sliced avocado
2 tomatoes, cut into ¼-inch dice
1 red onion, finely chopped
¼ cup mild to medium-hot prepared salsa
15-ounce can red kidney beans, rinsed and drained
4 cups torn iceberg lettuce
2 ounces baked tortilla chips

1. Preheat the oven to 400°. Rub the pork with the cumin, chili powder, and ¼ teaspoon of the salt. Place the pork in a small roasting pan and roast for 25 minutes, or until cooked through but still juicy. Place the pork on a plate and let it stand for 10 minutes. Thinly slice the pork, reserving any juices on the plate.

2. Meanwhile, in a large bowl, with a potato masher or the back of a spoon, mash the peas and avocado until not quite smooth, with some texture remaining. Stir in half of the tomatoes, the onion, salsa, kidney beans, pork juices, and the remaining ¼ teaspoon salt.

3. Line 4 plates with the lettuce and place the avocado mixture and the sliced pork over. Sprinkle with the remaining tomatoes and the tortilla chips and serve warm or at room temperature.

Helpful hint: If you have a cutting board with a well or channel to collect the juices, you can transfer the pork directly to the cutting board, rather than to a plate, to let it stand before slicing.

FAT: 7G/21%
CALORIES: 298
SATURATED FAT: 1.2G
CARBOHYDRATE: 38G
PROTEIN: 23G
CHOLESTEROL: 37MG
SODIUM: 558MG

In considerably less time than it takes to cook a pot of rice, you can have a steaming bowl of spiced couscous, laced with lemon and tossed with chopped apricots and pecans, ready to serve. More the consistency of a pasta than a grain, quick-cooking couscous is the ideal companion for quickly broiled meat, such as this juicy medium-rare beef.

SPICY BEEF SALAD WITH APRICOT-PECAN COUSCOUS

SERVES: 4
WORKING TIME: 15 MINUTES
TOTAL TIME: 30 MINUTES

1 teaspoon paprika

¾ teaspoon ground cumin

¾ teaspoon ground coriander

¾ teaspoon salt

½ teaspoon ground ginger

½ teaspoon freshly ground black pepper

10 ounces well-trimmed top round of beef

¾ teaspoon grated lemon zest

3 tablespoons fresh lemon juice

1 tablespoon olive oil

1½ cups couscous (see tip)

2½ cups reduced-sodium chicken broth, defatted

½ cup dried apricots, cut into ¼-inch dice

¼ cup coarsely chopped pecans

4 scallions, thinly sliced

4 cups mixed torn greens

1. Preheat the broiler. In a large heatproof bowl, combine the paprika, cumin, coriander, salt, ginger, and pepper. Remove 1½ teaspoons of the spice mixture and rub it into the meat. Broil the meat 6 inches from the heat for about 3½ minutes per side, or until medium-rare. Place the beef on a plate and let it stand for 10 minutes. Thinly slice the beef on the diagonal, reserving any juices on the plate.

2. Meanwhile, add the lemon zest, lemon juice, and oil to the spice mixture remaining in the bowl. Add the couscous, stirring to combine. In a small saucepan, bring the broth, apricots, and 1 cup of water to a boil over medium heat. Pour over the couscous, cover, and let stand until most of the liquid has been absorbed and the couscous is tender, about 5 minutes.

3. Stir the beef juices, pecans, and scallions into the couscous. Line 4 plates with the greens, top with the couscous, arrange the sliced beef alongside, and serve warm or at room temperature.

Helpful hint: Store pecans and other nuts in airtight containers in the freezer. Rich in oils, nuts spoil easily.

TIP

Traditional North African couscous takes a long time and quite a bit of work to prepare. But couscous found in supermarkets is precooked and requires only steeping. Fluff the softened couscous with a fork, which will separate the grains without crushing them.

FAT: 11G/20%
CALORIES: 501
SATURATED FAT: 1.8G
CARBOHYDRATE: 69G
PROTEIN: 30G
CHOLESTEROL: 45MG
SODIUM: 822MG

HAM AND SWEET POTATO SALAD

SERVES: 4
WORKING TIME: 15 MINUTES
TOTAL TIME: 25 MINUTES

1 pound sweet potatoes, peeled and cut into ½-inch cubes

½ pound all-purpose potatoes, peeled and cut into ½-inch cubes

½ cup reduced-sodium chicken broth, defatted

¼ cup frozen apple juice concentrate, thawed

2 tablespoons balsamic vinegar

2½ teaspoons Dijon mustard

¾ teaspoon ground ginger

2 ripe pears, peeled, cored, and cut into ½-inch cubes

2 ribs celery, thinly sliced

1½ cups frozen peas, thawed

½ pound thinly sliced baked ham, slivered

1. In a large pot of boiling water, cook the sweet potatoes and all-purpose potatoes until firm-tender, about 10 minutes. Drain.

2. Meanwhile, in a large bowl, combine the broth, apple juice concentrate, vinegar, mustard, and ginger. Add the cooked potatoes, tossing gently to coat. Add the pears, celery, peas, and ham, tossing to combine. Divide among 4 plates and serve warm, at room temperature, or chilled.

Helpful hint: You have lots of options for varying this salad: Try apples instead of pears, fennel in place of celery, or asparagus tips instead of peas.

FAT: 4G/11%
CALORIES: 332
SATURATED FAT: 1.1G
CARBOHYDRATE: 57G
PROTEIN: 18G
CHOLESTEROL: 30MG
SODIUM: 924MG

R*ibbons of baked ham mingle with sweet and white potatoes, pears, celery, and peas for a colorful, confetti-like salad. The tangy dressing features the warming flavors of mustard and ginger. Delicious warm, at room temperature, or chilled, this salad makes a great second-day lunch if you have some left over. Serve the salad with whole-grain rolls or crunchy bread sticks.*

BEEF-BARLEY SALAD

SERVES: 4
WORKING TIME: 20 MINUTES
TOTAL TIME: 30 MINUTES

Whether in a salad or a soup, beef and barley are a winning combination. Here, the two are tossed with crisp fresh vegetables and pecans.

10 ounces well-trimmed flank steak

½ teaspoon salt

¼ cup fresh lemon juice

2½ cups reduced-sodium chicken broth, defatted

3 cloves garlic, minced

1 teaspoon grated lemon zest

½ teaspoon ground ginger

1½ cups quick-cooking barley

6 ounces green beans, cut into 1-inch lengths

2 teaspoons olive oil

2 carrots, shredded

2 tomatoes, cut into 8 wedges each

2 tablespoons coarsely chopped pecans (½ ounce)

4 cups torn romaine lettuce leaves

1. Preheat the broiler. Rub the steak with the salt and 1 tablespoon of the lemon juice. Broil 6 inches from the heat for about 3½ minutes per side, or until medium-rare. Place the steak on a plate and let it stand for 10 minutes. Cut the steak into bite-size pieces, reserving any juices on the plate.

2. Meanwhile, in a medium saucepan, combine 2 cups of the broth, ½ cup of water, the garlic, lemon zest, and ginger and bring to a boil over medium heat. Add the barley, reduce to a simmer, cover, and cook until the barley is almost tender, about 8 minutes. Add the green beans and cook until the beans are crisp-tender and the barley is tender, about 3 minutes. Remove from the heat; do not drain any remaining liquid.

3. In a large bowl, combine the remaining ½ cup broth, the remaining 3 tablespoons lemon juice, the steak juices, and the oil. Add the beef, the barley mixture, carrots, tomatoes, and pecans to the bowl with the dressing, tossing well to combine.

4. Line 4 plates with the lettuce leaves and top with the beef and barley mixture. Serve warm, at room temperature, or chilled.

Helpful hint: If you're serving this salad chilled, don't spoon the beef and barley mixture onto the lettuce until just before serving.

FAT: 11G/24%
CALORIES: 415
SATURATED FAT: 2.9G
CARBOHYDRATE: 55G
PROTEIN: 26G
CHOLESTEROL: 36MG
SODIUM: 694MG

PO' BOY SALAD WITH CAJUN SEASONING

SERVES: 4
WORKING TIME: 15 MINUTES
TOTAL TIME: 25 MINUTES

1 teaspoon dried oregano

¼ teaspoon salt

½ teaspoon dried thyme

¼ teaspoon cayenne pepper

¼ teaspoon freshly ground
black pepper

10 ounces well-trimmed flank
steak

¼ cup fresh lime juice

½ cup reduced-sodium chicken
broth, defatted

1 tablespoon chili sauce

2 teaspoons Dijon mustard

19-ounce can chick-peas, rinsed
and drained

1 cup cherry tomatoes, halved

1 red onion, halved and thinly
sliced

Four 6-inch pita breads, each
cut into 6 wedges

4 cups mixed torn greens

1. Preheat the broiler. In a small bowl, combine the oregano, salt, thyme, cayenne, and black pepper. Sprinkle the steak with 2 tablespoons of the lime juice. Sprinkle with the herb mixture, rubbing it in. Broil the steak 6 inches from the heat for about 3½ minutes per side, or until medium-rare. Place the beef on a plate and let it stand for 10 minutes. Thinly slice the beef on the diagonal, reserving any juices on the plate.

2. Meanwhile, in a medium bowl, combine the broth, chili sauce, mustard, and the remaining 2 tablespoons lime juice. Stir in the beef juices. Add the sliced beef, the chick-peas, tomatoes, onion, pita bread, and greens, tossing to combine. Divide among 4 plates and serve warm, at room temperature, or chilled.

Helpful hints: Crisp yet tender greens work well in this salad—baby romaine, or green or red leaf lettuce, are good choices. If you're serving this salad chilled, don't add the greens or pita bread to the other ingredients until just before serving.

FAT: 9G/20%
CALORIES: 415
SATURATED FAT: 2.5G
CARBOHYDRATE: 57G
PROTEIN: 27G
CHOLESTEROL: 36MG
SODIUM: 859MG

A *po' boy is the New Orleans version of a hero sandwich. This po' boy salad is packed with flavor.*

Down-Home Pork Salad

SERVES: 4
WORKING TIME: 15 MINUTES
TOTAL TIME: 50 MINUTES

Here's a great choice for a potluck supper—a refreshing change from heavier fare, but straightforward and familiar enough to appeal to everyone. The chunks of pork and potato are balanced by crisp celery, scallions, and bell peppers; the dressing is a lemony blend of reduced-fat mayonnaise and nonfat yogurt. A border of tomato gives the salad a festive air.

¾ pound well-trimmed pork tenderloin

¾ teaspoon salt

½ teaspoon freshly ground black pepper

1½ pounds red potatoes, cut into eighths

½ cup plain nonfat yogurt

2 tablespoons reduced-fat mayonnaise

½ teaspoon grated lemon zest

2 tablespoons fresh lemon juice

3 ribs celery, thinly sliced

3 scallions, cut into ½-inch lengths

2 yellow or red bell peppers, cut into ½-inch squares

4 tomatoes, cut into 4 slices each

1. Preheat the oven to 400°. Sprinkle the pork with ¼ teaspoon of the salt and ¼ teaspoon of the black pepper. Place the pork in a baking dish or small roasting pan and roast until the pork is cooked through, about 30 minutes. Place the pork on a plate and let it stand for 10 minutes. Thinly slice the pork, then cut it into bite-size pieces, reserving any juices on the plate.

2. Meanwhile, in a medium pot of boiling water, cook the potatoes until tender, about 12 minutes. Drain. In a large bowl, combine the yogurt, mayonnaise, lemon zest, lemon juice, pork juices, the remaining ½ teaspoon salt, and remaining ¼ teaspoon black pepper. Add the cooked potatoes, tossing to coat.

3. Add the pork, celery, scallions, and bell peppers to the bowl, tossing gently to combine. Line a platter with the tomato slices, top with the salad mixture, and serve at room temperature or chilled.

Helpful hint: If you're making the salad ahead of time to serve it chilled, don't arrange the salad over the tomatoes until just before serving.

FAT: 6G/17%
CALORIES: 325
SATURATED FAT: 1.4G
CARBOHYDRATE: 45G
PROTEIN: 25G
CHOLESTEROL: 51MG
SODIUM: 582MG

Although it centers on country-style oven-barbecued pork, there's quite a bit of subtle sophistication in this dish. The rich, warm flavors of the pork are poised against the assertive bite of watercress; the greens are dotted with crisp, colorful corn, bell pepper, and red onion. The chili dressing is spiked with a jolt of lime juice. Serve the salad with warm garlic bread.

OVEN-BARBECUED PORK WITH CORN-WATERCRESS SALAD

SERVES: 4
WORKING TIME: 15 MINUTES
TOTAL TIME: 55 MINUTES

2 cloves garlic, peeled

½ cup chili sauce

½ cup jarred roasted red peppers, rinsed and drained

2 tablespoons chopped yellow onion

1 tablespoon molasses

2 teaspoons firmly packed light brown sugar

¾ pound well-trimmed pork tenderloin

3 tablespoons fresh lime juice

1 green bell pepper, cut into ½-inch squares

1 red onion, cut into ½-inch cubes

1½ cups frozen corn kernels, thawed

4 cups watercress, tough stems removed (see tip)

1. Preheat the oven to 400°. In a small pot of boiling water, cook the garlic for 2 minutes to blanch. In a food processor, combine the garlic, chili sauce, roasted peppers, yellow onion, molasses, and brown sugar and process until smooth. Measure out 3 tablespoons of the chili sauce mixture and transfer the remainder to a medium bowl.

2. Rub the pork with the reserved 3 tablespoons chili sauce mixture. Place the pork in a baking dish or small roasting pan and roast for about 25 minutes, or until cooked through but still juicy. Place the pork on a plate and let it stand for 10 minutes. Thinly slice the pork crosswise, then cut each slice into ½-inch chunks, reserving any juices on the plate.

3. Meanwhile, add the lime juice to the chili sauce mixture in the bowl, stirring to combine. Fold in the bell pepper, red onion, corn, and watercress, tossing to combine.

4. Spoon the corn mixture onto 4 plates, top with the pork and juices, and serve warm, at room temperature, or chilled.

Helpful hints: Tart-bitter greens make a big flavor impact in this salad; instead of watercress, you could use chicory or arugula. If you're serving the salad chilled, don't arrange the pork slices over the corn mixture until just before serving.

FAT: 4G/14%
CALORIES: 256
SATURATED FAT: 1.1G
CARBOHYDRATE: 36G
PROTEIN: 23G
CHOLESTEROL: 50MG
SODIUM: 552MG

TIP

Holding each branch of watercress by the stem, pull off the smaller sprigs of tender leaves; discard the thick stems.

STIR-FRIED PORK AND RICE SALAD

SERVES: 4
WORKING TIME: 15 MINUTES
TOTAL TIME: 35 MINUTES

Here's a new way to serve a stir-fry: as a salad (warm or chilled) with the rice stirred right in. The healthful balance of grain, vegetables, and lean meat is enhanced with a tomato-soy dressing. The pork strips, dredged with seasoned flour, develop a thin, tender crust as they cook. You can make the dish with brown rice, but you'll need to allow some extra cooking time.

1⅓ cups long-grain rice

3 cloves garlic, minced

¾ teaspoon ground ginger

½ teaspoon salt

3 carrots, halved lengthwise and thinly sliced

6 ounces mushrooms, thinly sliced

⅓ cup ketchup

¼ cup rice vinegar

2 tablespoons reduced-sodium soy sauce

2 tablespoons flour

½ teaspoon ground coriander

10 ounces well-trimmed pork tenderloin, cut into 2 x ¼-inch matchsticks

1 tablespoon dark Oriental sesame oil

1½ cups frozen peas, thawed

2 ribs celery, halved lengthwise and thinly sliced

¼ cup coarsely chopped peanuts

1. In a medium saucepan, bring 3 cups of water to a boil. Add the rice, garlic, ginger, and ¼ teaspoon of the salt. Reduce to a simmer, cover, and cook until the rice is firm-tender, about 12 minutes. Add the carrots and mushrooms, stirring to combine; re-cover and cook until the rice is tender, about 7 minutes.

2. In a large bowl, combine the ketchup, vinegar, and soy sauce. Add the cooked rice mixture, tossing to coat.

3. On a sheet of waxed paper, combine the flour, coriander, and the remaining ¼ teaspoon salt. Dredge the pork in the flour mixture, shaking off the excess. In a large nonstick skillet, heat the sesame oil until hot but not smoking over medium heat. Add the pork and cook, stirring frequently, until lightly browned and cooked through, about 2 minutes.

4. Transfer the stir-fried pork to the bowl with the rice. Stir in the peas, celery, and peanuts. Divide the salad among 4 plates and serve at room temperature or chilled.

Helpful hints: This salad is a great candidate for make-ahead: It can be made up to 12 hours in advance and covered and refrigerated. For a change, try using cashews instead of peanuts.

FAT: 11G/19%
CALORIES: 518
SATURATED FAT: 2.1G
CARBOHYDRATE: 77G
PROTEIN: 27G
CHOLESTEROL: 46MG
SODIUM: 946MG

THAI-STYLE BEEF SALAD WITH NOODLES

SERVES: 4
WORKING TIME: 20 MINUTES
TOTAL TIME: 35 MINUTES

10 ounces well-trimmed beef sirloin

¼ teaspoon salt

8 ounces fettuccine

½ pound sugar snap peas or snow peas, strings removed

⅓ cup chili sauce

2 tablespoons fresh lime juice

2 tablespoons reduced-sodium soy sauce

4 teaspoons honey

½ teaspoon ground ginger

1½ cups cherry tomatoes, halved

4 scallions, thinly sliced on the diagonal

1 cucumber, peeled, halved lengthwise, seeded, and thinly sliced on the diagonal

8-ounce can crushed pineapple, drained

1. Preheat the broiler. Sprinkle the meat with ⅛ teaspoon of the salt. Broil 6 inches from the heat for about 3½ minutes per side, or until medium-rare. Place the beef on a plate and let it stand for 10 minutes. Thinly slice the beef on the diagonal, then cut it into bite-size pieces, reserving any juices on the plate.

2. Meanwhile, in a large pot of boiling water, cook the fettuccine until just tender. Add the sugar snap peas during the last 1 minute of cooking time. Drain well.

3. In a large bowl, combine the chili sauce, lime juice, soy sauce, honey, ginger, and the remaining ⅛ teaspoon salt. Add the sliced beef and juices, pasta, sugar snap peas, tomatoes, scallions, cucumber, and pineapple, tossing well to combine. Divide among 4 plates and serve at room temperature or chilled.

Helpful hint: To prepare the cucumber, peel it and halve it lengthwise, then scrape out the seeds using the tip of a teaspoon.

FAT: 7G/14%
CALORIES: 442
SATURATED FAT: 2G
CARBOHYDRATE: 69G
PROTEIN: 28G
CHOLESTEROL: 101MG
SODIUM: 793MG

148

The interplay of tastes and textures that characterizes Thai cooking is abundantly apparent in this salad. The velvety-smooth pasta ribbons are intertwined with succulent bite-size pieces of medium-rare sirloin; juicy tomatoes, crisp-tender sugar snap peas, and cucumber crescents contribute lots of fresh flavor. And as a sweet surprise, the salad includes shreds of pineapple.

We've expanded the concept of a French potato salad to create this appealing mixture of beef and vegetables. Red potatoes, cauliflower, green beans, and cherry tomatoes are combined with herbed broiled beef for a substantial dinner dish. Snippets of sun-dried tomato add sunny flavor. A warm baguette is a lovely accompaniment for this salad.

Marinated Vegetable and Beef Salad

Serves: 4
Working time: 20 minutes
Total time: 30 minutes

10 ounces well-trimmed top round of beef

½ teaspoon salt

½ teaspoon dried oregano

1 pound red potatoes, cut into ½-inch chunks

3 cups small cauliflower florets

½ pound green beans, cut into 1-inch lengths

½ cup sun-dried (not oil-packed) tomatoes, snipped into ½-inch pieces (see tip)

½ cup reduced-sodium chicken broth, defatted

2 tablespoons red wine vinegar

1 tablespoon olive oil

2 teaspoons Dijon mustard

½ teaspoon freshly ground black pepper

2 cups cherry tomatoes, halved

1. Preheat the broiler. Rub the beef with ¼ teaspoon of the salt and ¼ teaspoon of the oregano. Broil the beef 6 inches from the heat for about 3½ minutes per side, or until medium-rare. Place the beef on a plate and let it stand for 10 minutes. Thinly slice the beef on the diagonal, then cut it into bite-size pieces, reserving any juices on the plate.

2. Meanwhile, in a large pot of boiling water, cook the potatoes until firm-tender, about 10 minutes. Add the cauliflower, green beans, and sun-dried tomatoes during the last 4 minutes of cooking time. Drain well.

3. In a large bowl, combine the broth, vinegar, oil, mustard, pepper, the remaining ¼ teaspoon salt, and remaining ¼ teaspoon oregano. Add the cherry tomatoes, tossing to combine. Add the cooked potatoes, cauliflower, green beans, and sun-dried tomatoes, tossing to combine.

4. Add the meat and juices to the bowl with the vegetables, tossing well to combine. Serve warm, at room temperature, or chilled.

Helpful hint: If you have a cutting board with a well or channel to collect the juices, you can transfer the beef to the cutting board, rather than to a plate, to let it stand before slicing.

Fat: 6g/18%
Calories: 294
Saturated Fat: 1.3g
Carbohydrate: 37g
Protein: 24g
Cholesterol: 40mg
Sodium: 479mg

TIP

Sun-dried tomatoes are somewhat tough and leathery before they've been soaked, but it's easy to snip them into small pieces if you use kitchen scissors rather than a knife.

PORK SALAD WITH GREEN GODDESS DRESSING

SERVES: 4
WORKING TIME: 20 MINUTES
TOTAL TIME: 45 MINUTES

If food folklore is to be believed, this salad dressing is named after a play: During the run of "The Green Goddess" in San Francisco in the 1920s, a hotel chef created this recipe at the request of actor George Arliss, who was starring in the show. The heady herbal dressing is traditionally based on mayonnaise. Here, nonfat yogurt and reduced-fat sour cream are healthier stand-ins.

¾ pound well-trimmed pork tenderloin

¾ teaspoon salt

½ teaspoon freshly ground black pepper

4 medium all-purpose potatoes (1½ pounds total), quartered

½ cup reduced-sodium chicken broth, defatted

⅓ cup plain nonfat yogurt

¼ cup reduced-fat sour cream

2 tablespoons fresh lemon juice

1 teaspoon dried tarragon

2 tablespoons capers, rinsed and drained

2 tomatoes, cut into 8 wedges each

½ cup chopped fresh parsley

6 cups mixed torn greens

1. Preheat the oven to 400°. Sprinkle the pork with ½ teaspoon of the salt and ¼ teaspoon of the pepper. Place the pork in a baking dish or small roasting pan and roast for about 25 minutes, or until just cooked through. Place the pork on a plate and let it stand for 10 minutes. Thinly slice the pork, then cut it into bite-size pieces, reserving any juices on the plate.

2. Meanwhile, in a medium pot of boiling water, cook the potatoes until firm-tender, about 15 minutes. Drain, and when cool enough to handle, peel and cut into ½-inch chunks.

3. In a large bowl, combine the broth, yogurt, sour cream, lemon juice, tarragon, pork juices, the remaining ¼ teaspoon salt, and remaining ¼ teaspoon pepper. Fold in the cooked potatoes and capers, tossing well to coat. Add the pork, tomatoes, and parsley. Divide the greens among 4 plates, top with the pork mixture, and serve warm, at room temperature, or chilled.

Helpful hints: If you're serving the salad chilled, you can dress the potatoes and pork in advance, but don't add the tomatoes and parsley until serving time. Traditional Green Goddess salad is made with romaine, escarole, and chicory; you could use these to line the plate, or use green and red leaf lettuce.

FAT: 6G/17%
CALORIES: 311
SATURATED FAT: 2.1G
CARBOHYDRATE: 41G
PROTEIN: 26G
CHOLESTEROL: 61MG
SODIUM: 774MG

GLOSSARY

Balsamic vinegar—A dark red vinegar made from the unfermented juice of pressed grapes, most commonly the white Trebbiano, and aged in wooden casks. The authentic version is produced in a small region in Northern Italy, around Modena, and tastes richly sweet with a slight sour edge. Because this vinegar is so mild, you can make dressings and marinades with less oil.

Basil—A highly fragrant herb with a flavor somewhere between licorice and cloves. Like many fresh herbs, basil will retain more of its taste if added at the end of cooking; dried basil is quite flavorful and can stand up to longer cooking. Store fresh basil by placing the stems in a container of water and covering the leaves loosely with a plastic bag.

Beef, top and bottom round—The inside and outside portions of a cut of beef that comes from the hindquarters of a steer, just behind the loin. Top and bottom round are among the leanest cuts of beef, and are also relatively tender. These cuts are sold as roasts or steaks.

Cayenne pepper—A hot spice ground from dried red chili peppers. Add cayenne to taste when preparing Mexican, Tex-Mex, Indian, Chinese, and Caribbean dishes; start with just a small amount, as cayenne is fiery-hot.

Chili powder—A commercially prepared seasoning mixture made from ground dried chilies, oregano, cumin, coriander, salt, and dehydrated garlic, and sometimes cloves and allspice. Use in chilis, sauces, and spice rubs for a Southwestern punch. Chili powders can range in strength from mild to very hot; for proper potency, use within 6 months of purchase. Pure ground chili powder, without any added spices, is also available.

Cilantro/Coriander—A lacy-leaved green herb (called by both names). The plant's seeds are dried and used as a spice (known as coriander). The fresh herb, much used in Mexican and Asian cooking, looks like pale flat-leaf parsley and is strongly aromatic. Store fresh cilantro by placing the stems in a container of water and covering the leaves loosely with a plastic bag. Coriander seeds are important in Mexican and Indian cuisines; sold whole or ground, they have a somewhat citrusy flavor that complements both sweet and savory dishes.

Cornstarch—A fine flour made from the germ of the corn. Cornstarch, like flour, is used as a fat-free sauce thickener; cornstarch-thickened sauces are lighter, glossier, and more translucent than those made with flour. To prevent lumps, combine the cornstarch with a cold liquid before adding it to a hot sauce; bring it gently to a boil and don't stir too vigorously or the sauce may thin.

Cumin—A pungent, peppery-tasting spice essential to many Middle Eastern, Asian, Mexican, and Mediterranean dishes. Available ground or as whole seeds; the spice can be toasted in a dry skillet to bring out its flavor.

Fennel seeds—The seeds of the common fennel plant, which have a slightly sweet, licorice-like taste. Fennel seeds are often used to season Italian sausages, and are also used in pasta sauces and with seafood.

Flank steak—A relatively thin, very lean beef steak cut from just behind the belly. Flank steak is sold very well trimmed, and has relatively little interior fat. It can be broiled, but should not be cooked beyond medium-rare, as it can get tough.

Garlic—The edible bulb of a plant closely related to onions, leeks, and chives. Garlic can be pungently assertive or sweetly mild, depending on how it is prepared: Minced or crushed garlic yields a more powerful flavor than whole or halved cloves. Whereas sautéing turns garlic rich and savory, slow simmering or roasting produces a mild, mellow flavor. Select firm, plump heads with dry skins; avoid heads that have begun to sprout. Store garlic in an open or loosely covered container in a cool, dark place for up to 2 months.

Ginger, fresh—A thin-skinned root used as a seasoning. Fresh ginger adds sweet pungency to Asian and Indian dishes. Tightly wrapped, unpeeled fresh ginger can be refrigerated for 1 week or frozen for up to 6 months. Ground ginger is not a true substitute for fresh, but it will lend a warming flavor to soups, stews, and sauces.

Honey—A liquid sweetener made by honeybees from flower nectar. It ranges in flavor from mild (orange blossom) to very strong (buckwheat). Deliciously versatile, honey can sweeten savory sauces or fruit desserts. Store honey at room temperature. If it crystallizes, place the open jar in a pan of warm water for a few minutes; or microwave it for 10 to 15 seconds.

Hot pepper sauce—A highly incendiary sauce made from a variety of hot peppers flavored with vinegar and salt. This sauce comes into play in Caribbean and Tex-Mex dishes as well as Creole and Cajun cuisines. Use sparingly, drop by drop, to introduce a hot edge to any dish.

Italian seasoning—A prepared herb and spice mixture that includes dried basil and oregano, garlic, onion, and pepper; it may also contain marjoram, rosemary, sage, thyme, and/or red pepper flakes. Italian seasoning is a timesaver when you're making sauces and salad dressings.

Juice, citrus—The flavorful liquid component of oranges, lemon, limes, tangerines, and the like. Freshly squeezed citrus juice has an inimitable freshness that livens up low-fat foods. Frozen juice concentrates make a tangy base for sweet or savory sauces. An inexpensive hand reamer makes quick work of juicing citrus fruits.

Mint—A large family of herbs used to impart a refreshingly heady fragrance and cool after-taste to foods; the most common types are spearmint and peppermint. As with other fresh herbs, mint is best added toward the end of the cooking time. Dried mint is fairly intense, so a pinch goes a long way. Store fresh mint the same way as fresh cilantro.

Mushrooms—A type of fungus, available in a wide range of colors, flavors, and shapes. Today most supermarkets offer, in addition to white button mushrooms, a choice of "exotic" varieties, including portobellos, richly flavored with large, round, flat tops; and shiitakes, an Oriental variety with an intense, almost meaty taste. Choose fresh mushrooms with intact, unshriveled caps; for most varieties, the gills under the caps should be tightly closed. For concentrated flavor, try dried mushrooms, such as porcini or Polish mushrooms (sold in small plastic tubs); reconstitute in hot water before using.

Olive oil—A fragrant oil pressed from olives. Olive oil is one of the signature ingredients of Italian cuisine. This oil is rich in monounsaturated fats, which make it more healthful than butter and other solid shortenings. Olive oil comes in different grades, reflecting the method used to refine the oil and the resulting level of acidity. The finest, most expensive oil is cold-pressed extra-virgin, which should be reserved for flavoring salad dressings and other uncooked or lightly cooked foods. "Virgin" and "pure" olive oils are slightly more acidic with less olive flavor, and are fine for most types of cooking.

Oregano—A member of the mint family characterized by small, pointed green leaves. Prized for its pleasantly bitter taste, oregano is essential to many Mediterranean-style dishes and is used in Mexican cooking as well.

Paprika—A spice ground from a variety of red peppers and used in many traditional Hungarian and Spanish dishes. Paprika colors foods a characteristic brick-red and flavors dishes from sweet to spicy-hot, depending on the pepper potency. Like all pepper-based spices, paprika loses its color and flavor with time; check your supply and replace it if necessary.

Parmesan cheese—An intensely flavored hard grating cheese. Genuine Italian Parmesan, stamped "Parmigiano-Reggiano" on the rind, is produced in the Emilia-Romagna region, and tastes richly nutty with a slight sweetness. Buy Parmesan in chunks and grate it as needed for best flavor and freshness. For a fine, fluffy texture that melts into hot foods, grate the cheese in a hand-cranked grater.

Parsley—A popular herb available in two varieties. Curly parsley, with lacy, frilly leaves, is quite mild and is preferred for garnishing, while flat-leaf Italian parsley has a stronger flavor and is better for cooking. Store parsley as you would basil. Since fresh parsley is so widely available, there is really no reason to use dried, which has very little flavor.

Peppercorns, black—The whole dried berries of a tropical vine, *piper nigrum*. A touch of this hot, pungent seasoning enlivens just about any savory dish, and the flavor of freshly ground pepper is so superior to pre-ground that no cook should be without a pepper grinder filled with peppercorns.

Peppers, bell—Large, sweet members of the Capsicum family of vegetables. Green bell peppers are the most common; red peppers have ripened and are sweeter. You can also buy yellow, orange, purple, and brown bell peppers in some markets. Choose well-colored, firm peppers that are heavy for

their size; these will have thick, juicy flesh. Store peppers in a plastic bag in the refrigerator for up to a week. Before preparing bell peppers, remove the stem, ribs, and seeds.

Pork chops—Crosswise cuts of pork from the center-cut loin or boneless loin (rib chops come from the rib section of the loin). Both kinds of chops are sold with and without the bone.

Pork loin and tenderloin—The cuts of pork that come from the animal's back, behind the shoulder; they are the leanest cuts of pork. The loin (shown below), is a long, thick section sold bone-in, boneless, and boned and tied (for roasting or braising). The tenderloin is the choicest part of the loin—a long, narrow cylinder of meat that can be cooked whole, or cut into slices or cubes for various recipes.

Prosciutto—A salt-cured, air-dried Italian ham that originated in the area around the city of Parma. This dense-textured, intensely flavored ham is served as an appetizer with melon or figs and also used in cooking, often to flavor sauces. Prosciutto has been produced in the United States for years, but imported Italian prosciutto is also available; the finest is labeled "Prosciutto di Parma." Our recipes should be made with very thinly sliced prosciutto *crudo* (raw) rather than prosciutto *cotto* (cooked).

Red pepper flakes—A spice made from a variety of dried red chili peppers. Pepper flakes will permeate a stew or a casserole with a burst of heat and flavor during the cooking and eating. Begin with a small amount—you can always add more.

Rosemary—An aromatic herb with needle-like leaves and a sharp pine-citrus flavor. Rosemary's robust flavor complements lamb particularly well, and it stands up to long cooking better than most herbs. If you can't get fresh rosemary, use whole dried leaves, which retain the flavor of the fresh herb quite well. Crush or chop rosemary leaves with a mortar and pestle or a chef's knife.

Sage—An intensely fragrant herb with grayish-green leaves. Sage will infuse a dish with a pleasant, musty, mint taste; it's especially good with pork. In its dried form, sage is sold as whole leaves, ground, and in a fluffy "rubbed" version. For the best flavor from the dried herb, buy whole leaves and crush them yourself.

Scallions—Immature onions (also called green onions) with a mild and slightly sweet flavor. Both the white bulb and the green tops can be used in cooking; the green tops make an attractive garnish. To prepare, trim off the base of the bulb, or root end, and any withered ends of the green tops. Remove the outermost, thin skin from around the bulb. Cut the white portion from the green tops and use separately, or use together in the same dish.

Sesame oil, Oriental—A dark, polyunsaturated oil, pressed from toasted sesame seeds, used as a flavor enhancer in many Asian and Indian dishes. Do not confuse the Oriental oil with its lighter colored counterpart, which is cold-pressed from untoasted sesame seeds and has a nearly neutral flavor. Store sesame oil in the refrigerator for up to 6 months.

Sherry—A fortified wine, originally made in Spain but now produced elsewhere as well. Sherries range in sweetness from quite dry (labeled fino, manzanillo, or simply "dry") to medium-dry (labeled amontillado or "milk sherry") to sweet (oloroso, also called "cream" or "golden"). Use a dry sherry to add a fragrant bouquet to savory sauces.

Sirloin, beef—A cut of beef that comes from the rear part of the loin (the lower back). The lean, tender meat from the sirloin is sold mainly as steaks, such as sirloin pinbone, sirloin round bone, and top sirloin, but also as roasts.

Soy sauce, reduced-sodium—A condiment made from fermented soybeans, wheat, and salt used to add a salty, slightly sweet flavor to food. Soy sauce is especially at home in stir-fries and other Asian-style preparations. Keep in mind that reduced-sodium sauces add the same flavor but much less sodium.

Sugar snap peas—A type of sweet peas with edible pods. Developed in the 1970s, sugar snaps are a cross between regular peas and snow peas. Unlike snow peas, which are flat, sugar snaps are plump, with fully formed peas inside the pods. Before eating sugar snaps, pinch off the tips and remove the string that runs along both the front and back of the pod. Eat sugar snaps raw, or steam or blanch them very briefly.

Tarragon—A potent, sweet herb with a licorice- or anise-like taste; often used with chicken or fish. Dried tarragon loses its flavor quickly; check its potency by crushing a little between your fingers and sniffing for the strong aroma. As with most herbs, you may substitute 1 teaspoon dried for each tablespoon of fresh.

Vidalia onions—A variety of exceptionally sweet onion grown in Georgia. Vidalias are available mainly in late spring and early summer; they're great in salads and other uncooked dishes because they are so mild. Similar onions are Maui (from Hawaii) and Walla Walla (from Washington State).

Vinegar, cider—A vinegar made from fermented apple cider. This vinegar has a pleasantly fruity flavor, and works well in recipes made with apples, pears, or other fruit.

Vinegar, red wine—A vinegar made from red grape juice. Use red wine vinegar to spike sauté sauces and marinades, especially those that employ Italian or French flavors.

Vinegar, rice—A pale vinegar made from fermented rice, it is milder than most other types of vinegar. Its light, clean flavor is much favored in Asian cooking. Japanese rice vinegar is widely available; be sure to buy the unseasoned type.

Wine, dry white—A non-sweet alcoholic beverage made from fermented grape juice. White wine may be made from white grapes, or from red grapes with their skins and seeds removed. Dry white wine lends a unique fragrance and flavor to sauces. Avoid the so-called "cooking wines" sold in supermarkets: These are of poor quality and may have added salt. Instead, buy an inexpensive but drinkable white. Once opened, recork and refrigerate the bottle.

Worcestershire sauce—A richly savory condiment based on vinegar, molasses, garlic, anchovies, tamarind, and onion. It takes its name from Worcester, England, where it was first bottled. Worcestershire is frequently used with meat—as a table condiment and in sauces or marinades. If the bottle is kept tightly capped, this potent condiment will keep almost indefinitely at room temperature.

Zest, citrus—The thin, outermost colored part of the rind of citrus fruits that contains strongly flavored oils. Zest imparts an intense flavor that makes a refreshing contrast to the richness of meat, poultry, or fish. Remove the zest with a grater, citrus zester, or vegetable peeler; be careful to remove only the colored layer, not the bitter white pith beneath it.

INDEX

Time-Life Books is a division of Time Life Inc.

TIME LIFE INC.

PRESIDENT and CEO: George Artandi

TIME-LIFE BOOKS

PRESIDENT: John D. Hall
PUBLISHER/MANAGING EDITOR: Neil Kagan

GREAT TASTE~LOW FAT
Light Beef & Pork

DEPUTY EDITOR: Marion Ferguson Briggs
MARKETING DIRECTOR: Cheryl D. Eklind

Consulting Editor: Catherine Boland Hackett

Vice President, Director of Finance: Christopher Hearing
Vice President, Book Production: Marjann Caldwell
Director of Operations: Eileen Bradley
Director of Photography and Research: John Conrad Weiser
Director of Editorial Administration (Acting): Barbara Levitt
Production Manager: Marlene Zack
Quality Assurance Manager: James King
Library: Louise D. Forstall

Design for Great Taste~Low Fat by David Fridberg of
Miles Fridberg Molinaroli, Inc.

REBUS, INC.

PUBLISHER: Rodney M. Friedman
EDITORIAL DIRECTOR: Charles L. Mee

Editorial Staff for *Light Beef & Pork*
Director, Recipe Development and Photography: Grace Young
Editorial Director: Kate Slate
Senior Recipe Developer: Sandra Rose Gluck
Recipe Developer: Paul Piccuito
Writer: Bonnie J. Slotnick
Managing Editor: Julee Binder Shapiro
Editorial Assistant: James W. Brown, Jr.
Nutritionists: Hill Nutrition Associates

Art Director: Timothy Jeffs
Photographer: Lisa Koenig
Photographer's Assistants: Alix Berenberg, Katie Bleacher Everard,
    Petra Liebetanz
Food Stylists: Catherine Paukner, Karen Pickus
Assistant Food Stylists: Charles Davis, Tracy Donovan
Prop Stylist: Debrah Donahue
Prop Coordinator: Karin Martin

Library of Congress Cataloging-in-Publication Data

Light beef & pork.
   p.   cm. -- (Great taste, low fat)
Includes index.
ISBN 0-7835-4565-7
1. Cookery (Beef). 2. Cookery (Pork). 3. Low-fat diet--Recipes.
I. Time-Life Books. II. Series.
TX749.5.B43L54   1997
641.6'62--dc21
                                           97-3465
                                           CIP

OTHER PUBLICATIONS

COOKING
WEIGHT WATCHERS® SMART CHOICE RECIPE COLLECTION
WILLIAMS-SONOMA KITCHEN LIBRARY

DO IT YOURSELF
THE TIME-LIFE COMPLETE GARDENER
HOME REPAIR AND IMPROVEMENT
THE ART OF WOODWORKING
FIX IT YOURSELF

TIME-LIFE KIDS
FAMILY TIME BIBLE STORIES
LIBRARY OF FIRST QUESTIONS AND ANSWERS
A CHILD'S FIRST LIBRARY OF LEARNING
I LOVE MATH
NATURE COMPANY DISCOVERIES
UNDERSTANDING SCIENCE & NATURE

HISTORY
THE AMERICAN STORY
VOICES OF THE CIVIL WAR
THE AMERICAN INDIANS
LOST CIVILIZATIONS
MYSTERIES OF THE UNKNOWN
TIME FRAME
THE CIVIL WAR
CULTURAL ATLAS

SCIENCE/NATURE
VOYAGE THROUGH THE UNIVERSE

*For information on and a full description of any of the Time-Life Books series
listed above, please call 1-800-621-7026 or write:*
Reader Information
Time-Life Customer Service
P.O. Box C-32068
Richmond, Virginia 23261-2068

METRIC CONVERSION CHARTS

VOLUME EQUIVALENTS
(fluid ounces/milliliters and liters)

US	Metric
1 tsp	5 ml
1 tbsp (½ fl oz)	15 ml
¼ cup (2 fl oz)	60 ml
⅓ cup	80 ml
½ cup (4 fl oz)	120 ml
⅔ cup	160 ml
¾ cup (6 fl oz)	180 ml
1 cup (8 fl oz)	240 ml
1 qt (32 fl oz)	950 ml
1 qt + 3 tbsps	1 L
1 gal (128 fl oz)	4 L

Conversion formula
Fluid ounces X 30 = milliliters
1000 milliliters = 1 liter

WEIGHT EQUIVALENTS
(ounces and pounds/grams and kilograms)

US	Metric
¼ oz	7 g
½ oz	15 g
¾ oz	20 g
1 oz	30 g
8 oz (½ lb)	225 g
12 oz (¾ lb)	340 g
16 oz (1 lb)	455 g
35 oz (2.2 lbs)	1 kg

Conversion formula
Ounces X 28.35 = grams
1000 grams = 1 kilogram

LINEAR EQUIVALENTS
(inches and feet/centimeters and meters)

US	Metric
¼ in	.75 cm
½ in	1.5 cm
¾ in	2 cm
1 in	2.5 cm
6 in	15 cm
12 in (1 ft)	30 cm
39 in	1 m

Conversion formula
Inches X 2.54 = centimeters
100 centimeters = 1 meter

TEMPERATURE EQUIVALENTS
(Fahrenheit/Celsius)

US	Metric
0° (freezer temperature)	-18°
32° (water freezes)	0°
98.6°	37°
180° (water simmers*)	82°
212° (water boils*)	100°
250° (low oven)	120°
350° (moderate oven)	175°
425° (hot oven)	220°
500° (very hot oven)	260°

*at sea level

Conversion formula
Degrees Fahrenheit minus
32 ÷ 1.8 = degrees Celsius